# Necropolises of New Orleans II

## A TRAVEL PHOTO ART BOOK

## LAINE CUNNINGHAM

Necropolises of New Orleans II
A Travel Photo Art Book

Published by Sun Dogs Creations
*Changing the World One Book at a Time*
ISBN: 9781946732231

Softcover Edition

Cover Design by Angel Leya

Copyright © 2017 Laine Cunningham

# Introduction

In New Orleans, the Cities of the Dead are beautiful, historic places to roam. The styles and sculptures decorating the crypts and mausoleums often reflect activities the interred individuals pursued during their lives. Many of the tombs hold multiple bodies, and the remains eventually end up jumbled together in the lower vault.

Visitors who wander through cemeteries on November 1, All Saints' Day, might witness families tidying up the graves and placing flowers, candles, or other decorations at their entrances. During other times of the year, mementos and decorative elements added to the gravesites make every visit moving.

These photos were taken at various cemeteries in New Orleans. They have been reproduced at the size of a standard cellphone screen to replicate a visit to these beautiful, touching, and meditative places. Just as you would with a phone, at times you'll need to rotate the book to view the *Necropolises of New Orleans II.*

# TEMPLE DWELLING

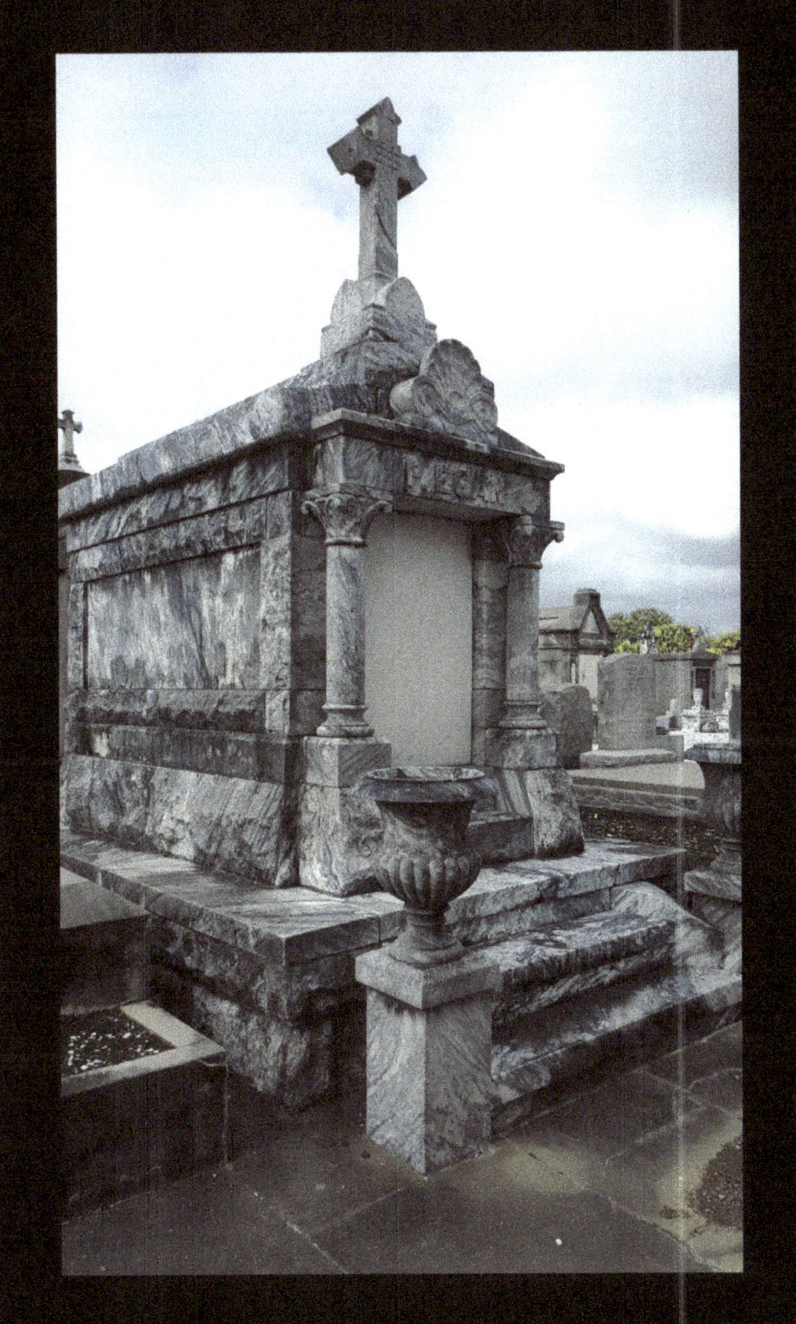

CHARLES AND EMMA

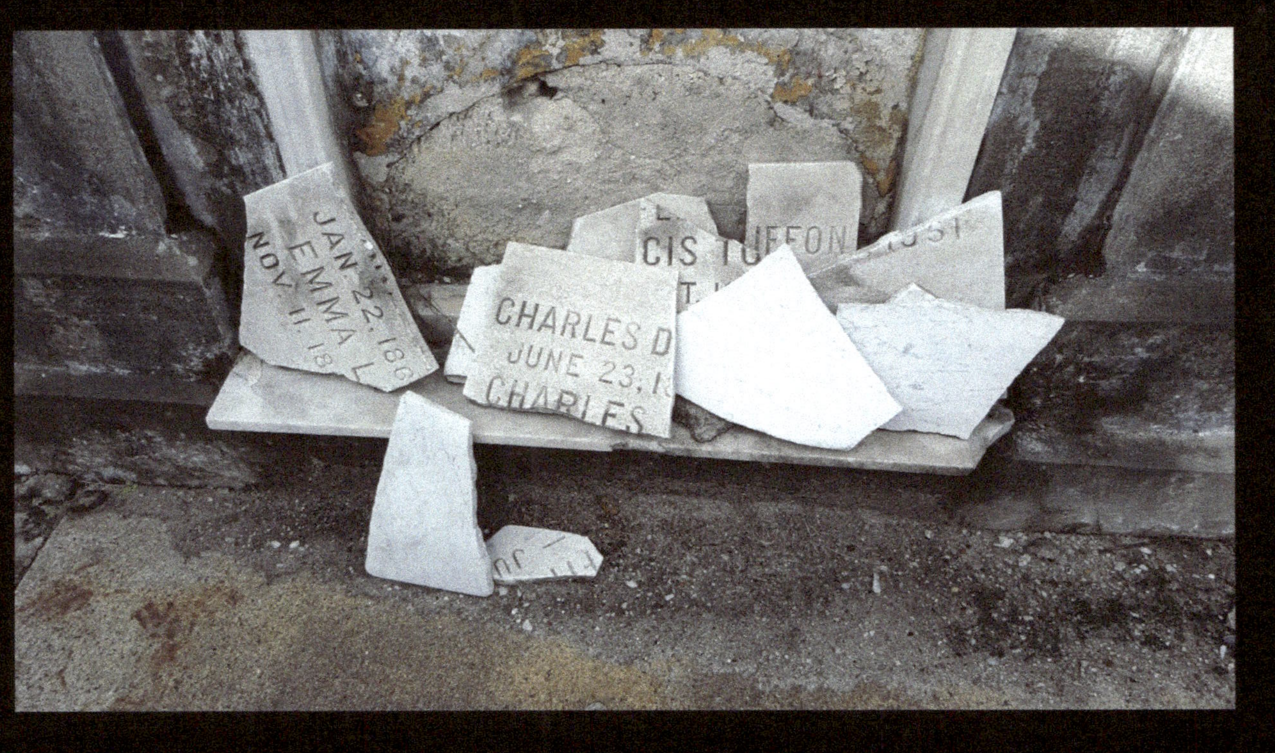
JAN. 22. 186
EMMA L.
NOV. 11. 18
CHARLES D
JUNE 23, 1
CHARLES
CIS TUFFON
FE. JU

# LAGRANGE TERRACE
# AT LAFAYETTE

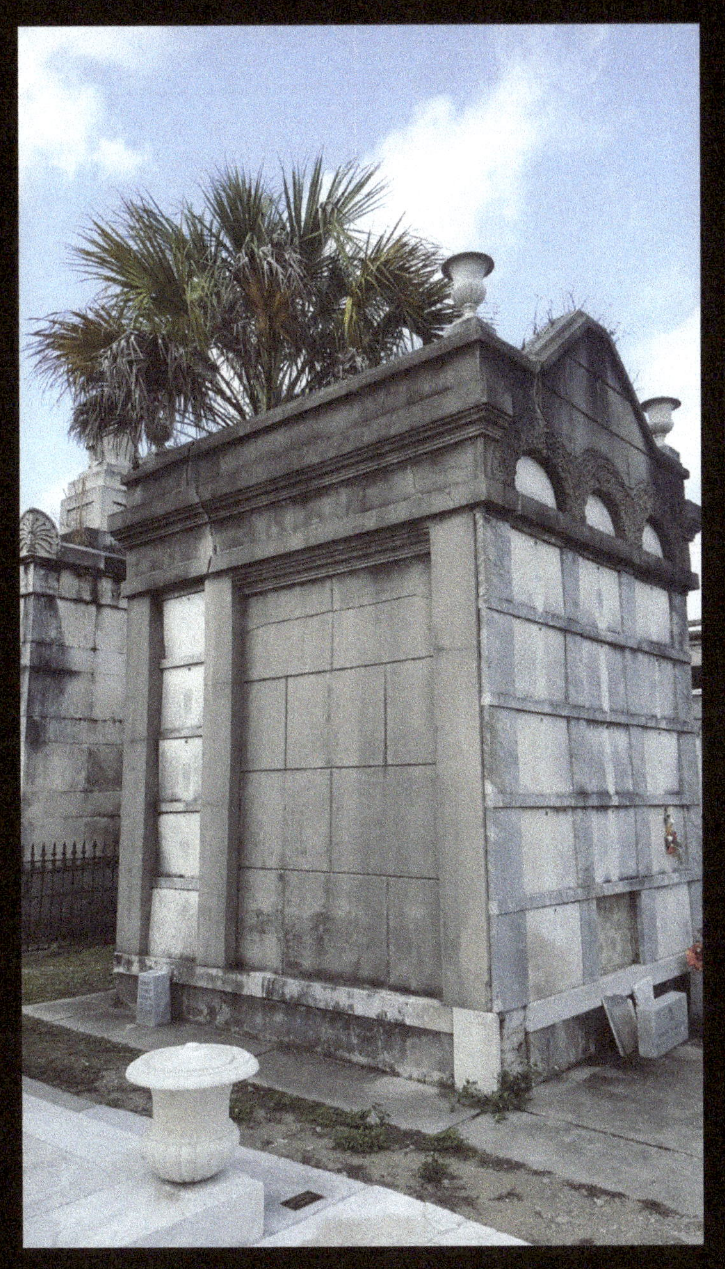

MIDDEN WITH SHELLS

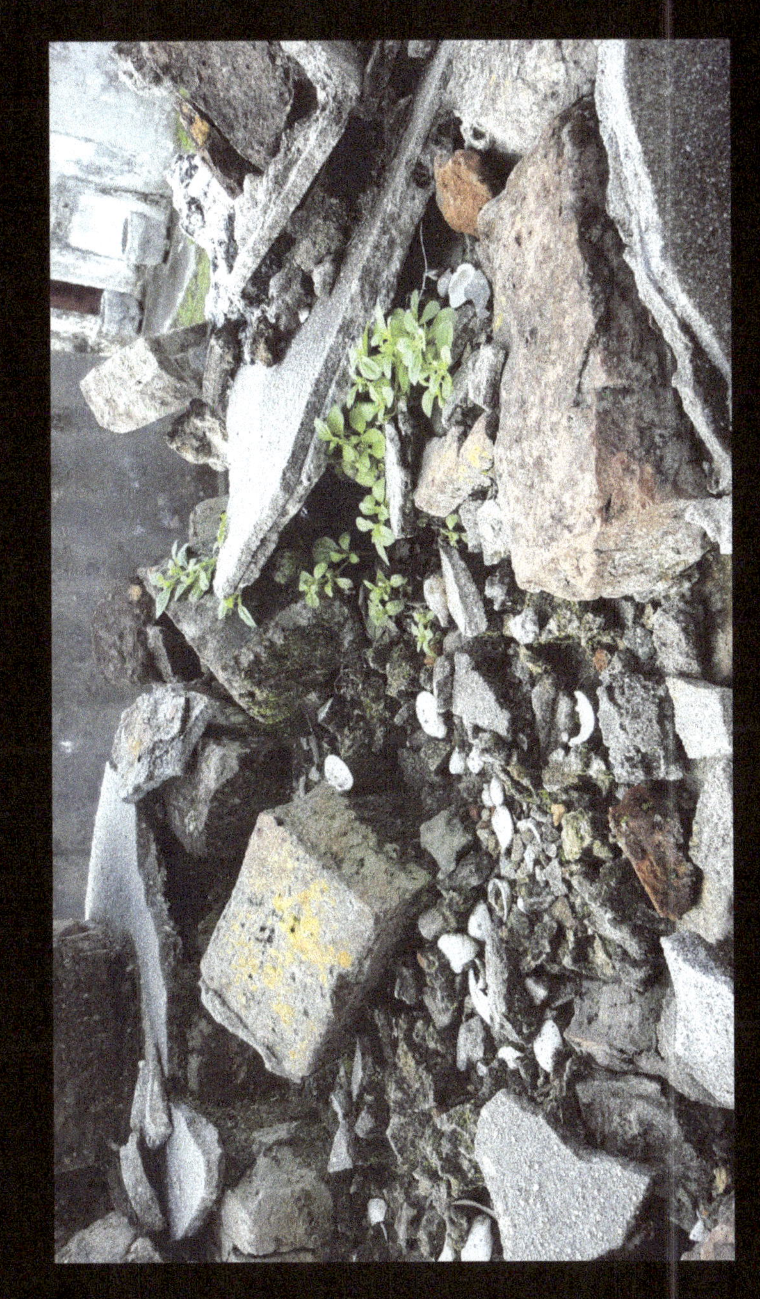

# FIELD OF CROSSES

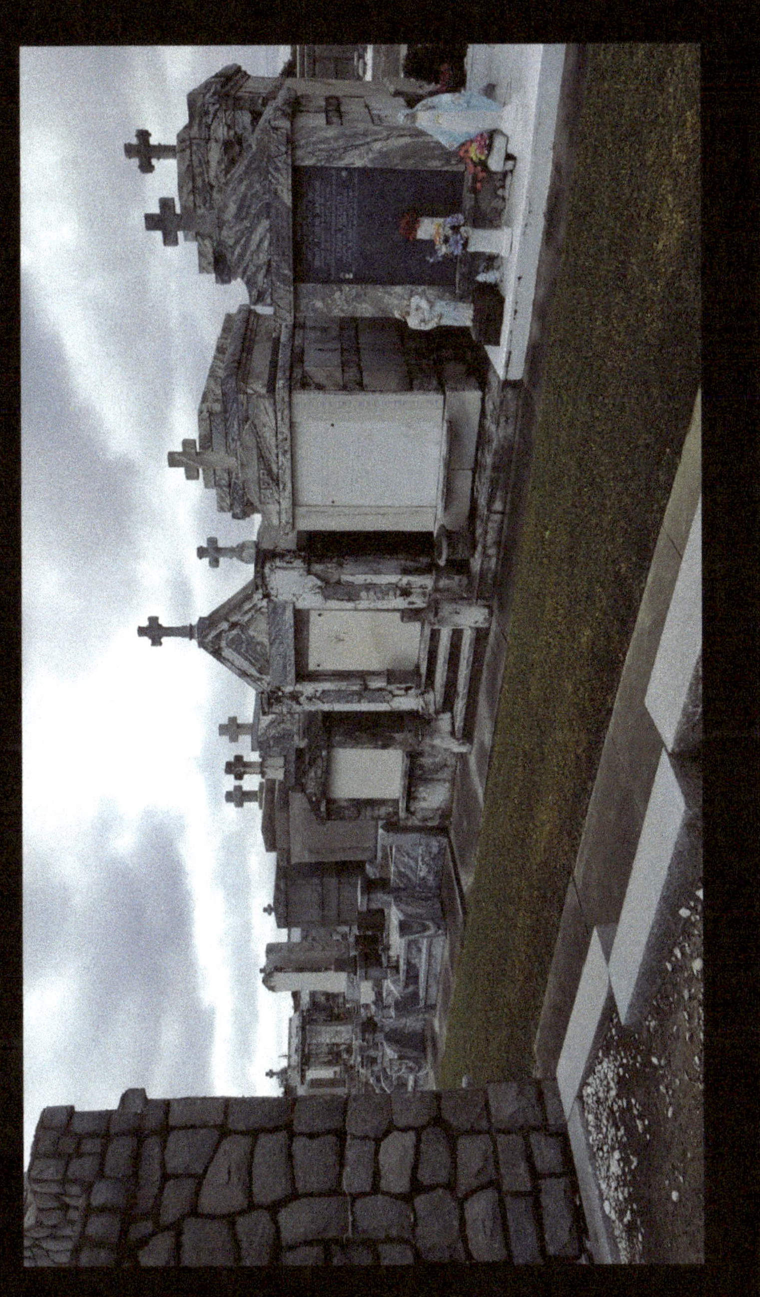

BASEMENT

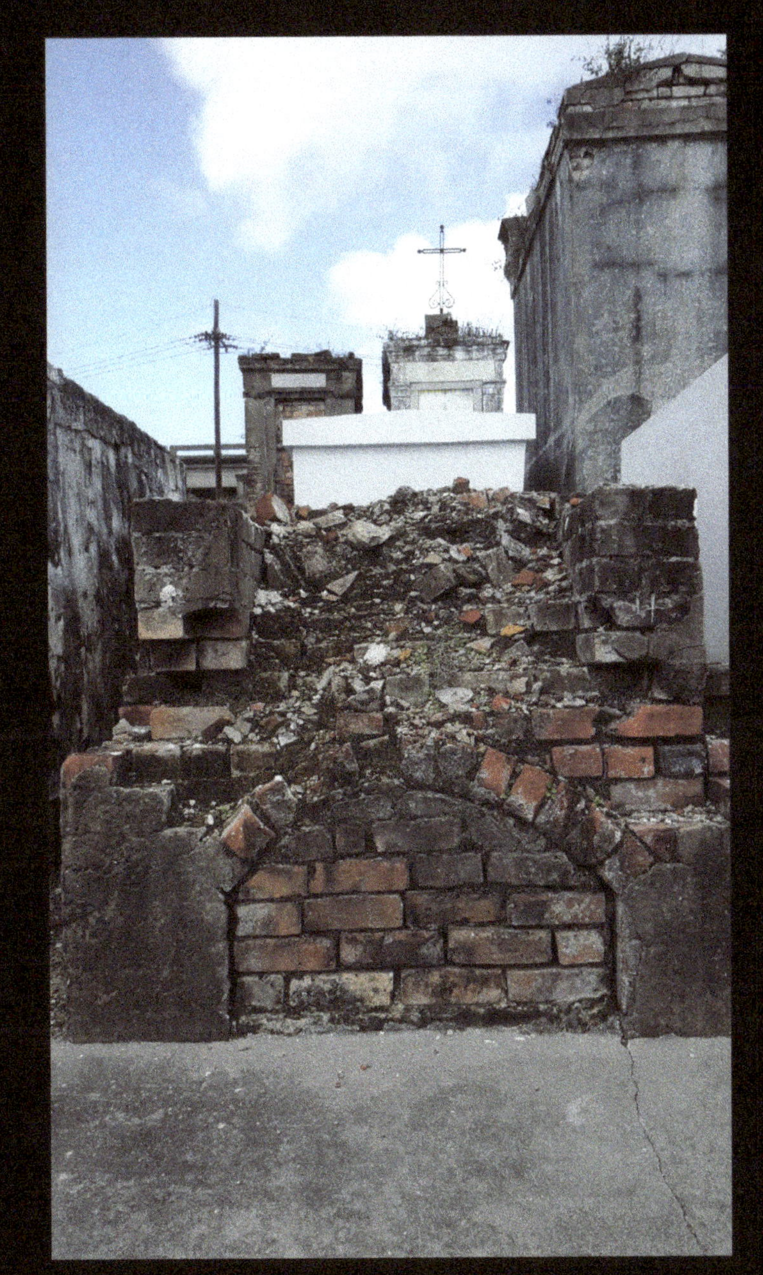

FARMSTEAD

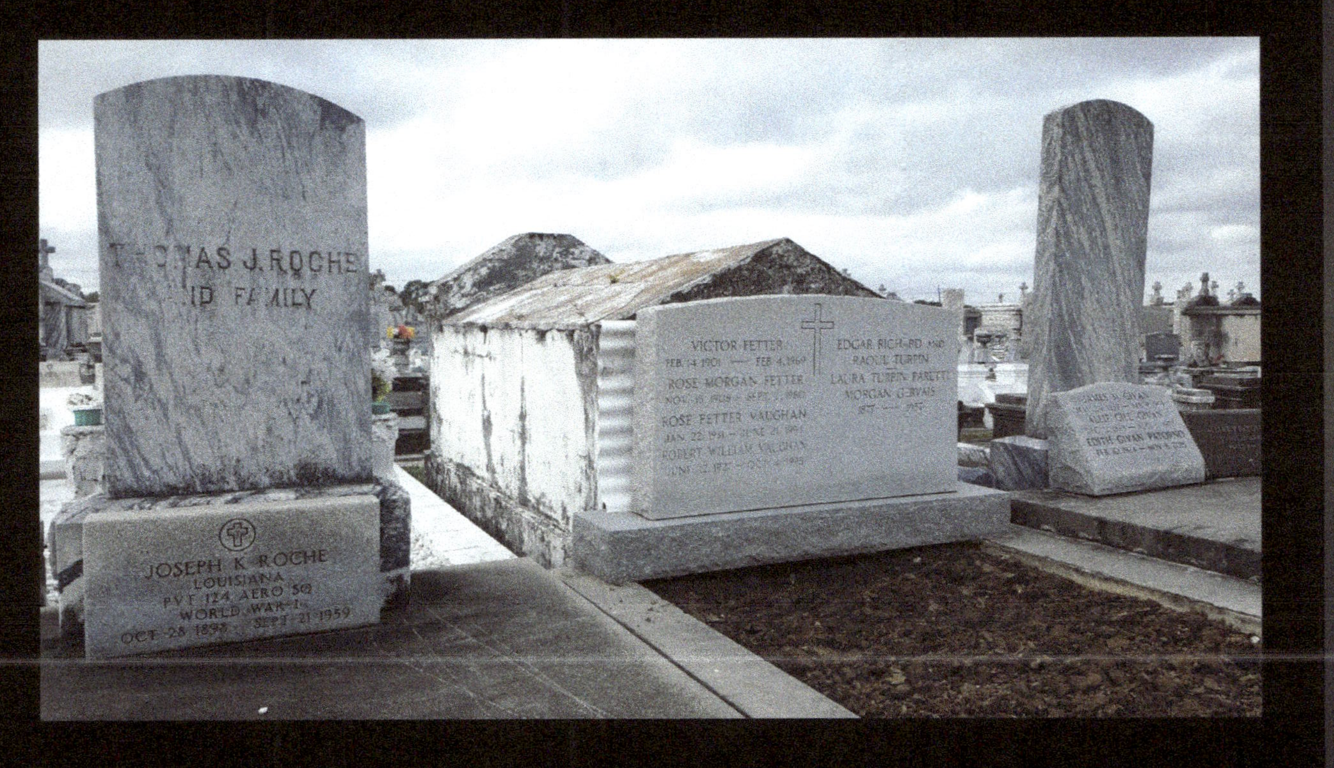

THOMAS J. ROCHE
AND FAMILY

JOSEPH K. ROCHE
LOUISIANA
PVT 124 AERO SQ
WORLD WAR I
OCT 28 1898    SEPT 21 1959

VICTOR FETTER
FEB 14 1901 — FEB 4 1969
ROSE MORGAN FETTER
NOV 18 1909 — SEPT 7 1980
ROSE FETTER VAUGHAN
JAN 22 1941 — JUNE 21 1961
ROBERT WILLIAM VAUGHAN
JUNE 22 1972 — OCT 4 1989

EDGAR RICHARD AND
RAOUL TURPIN
LAURA TURPIN PARETTI
MORGAN GERVAIS
1877 — 1955

# APOCALYPTIC LOVE

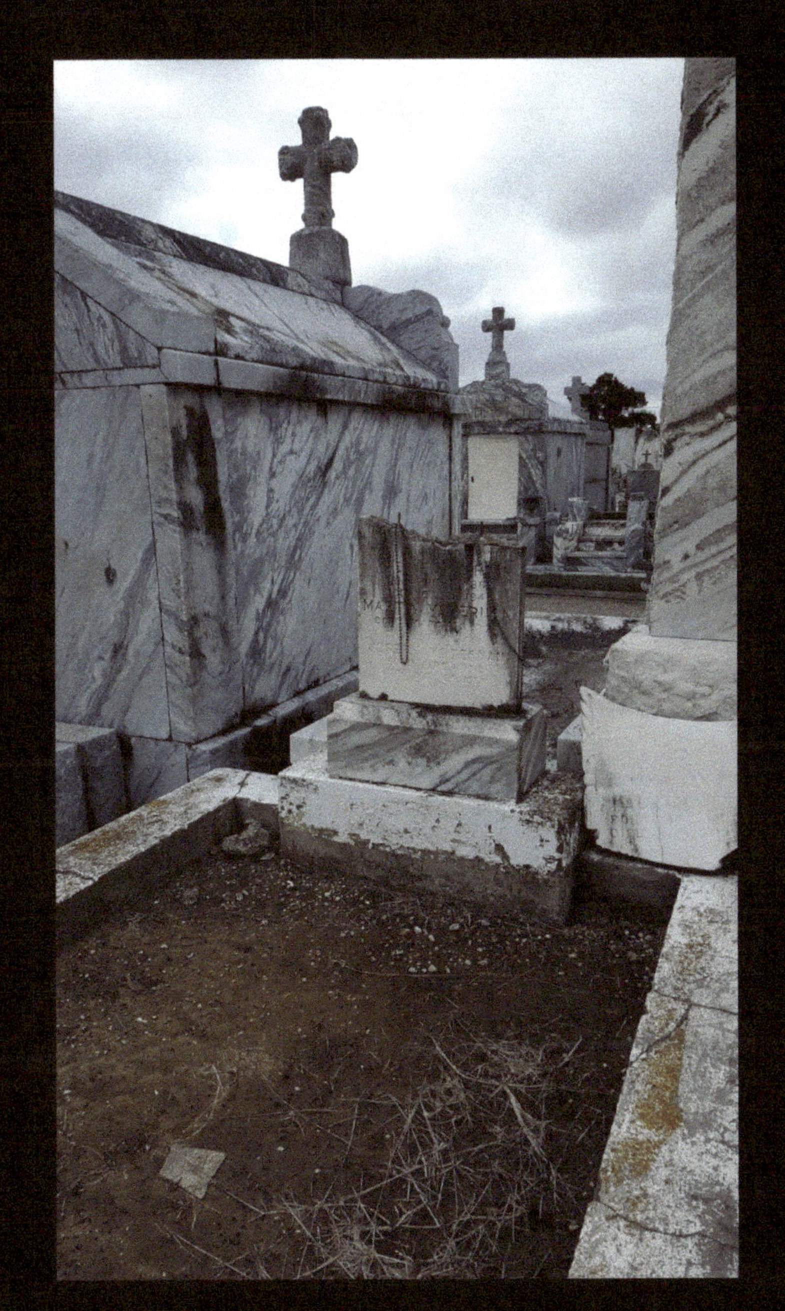

PLINTH

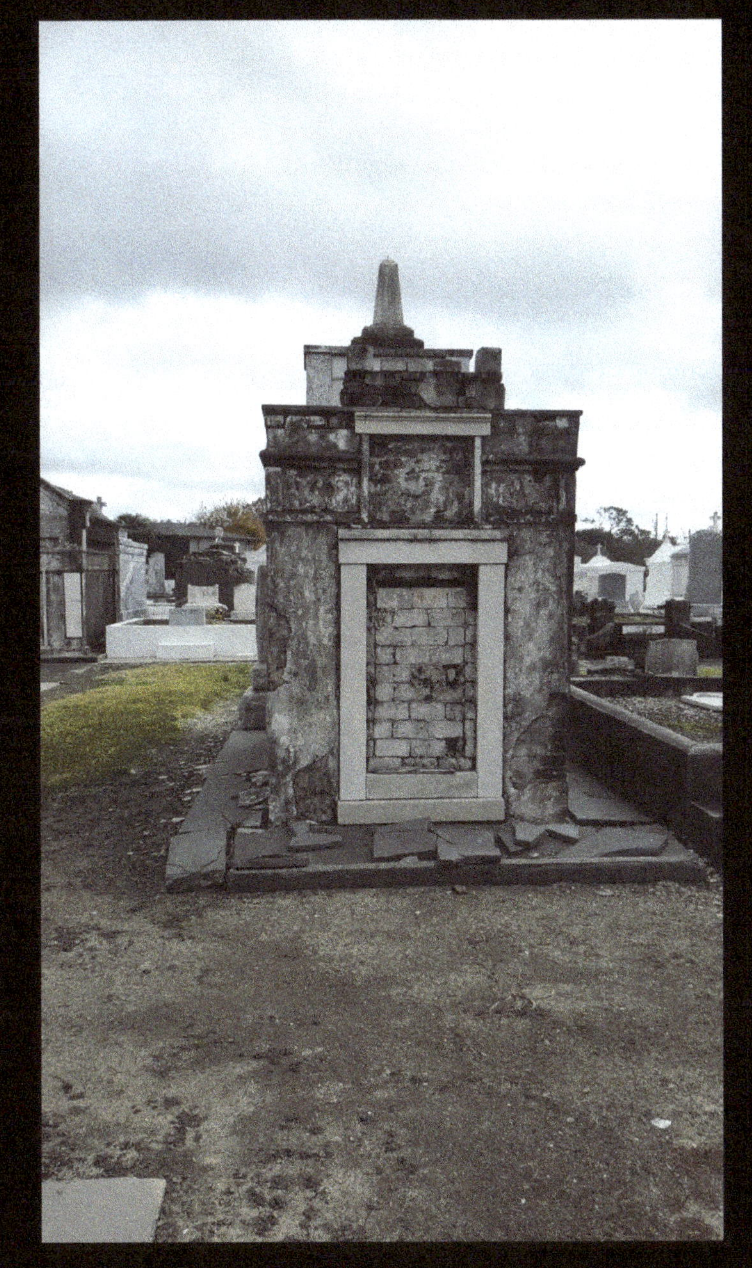

# LABOSTRIE'S DAISIES

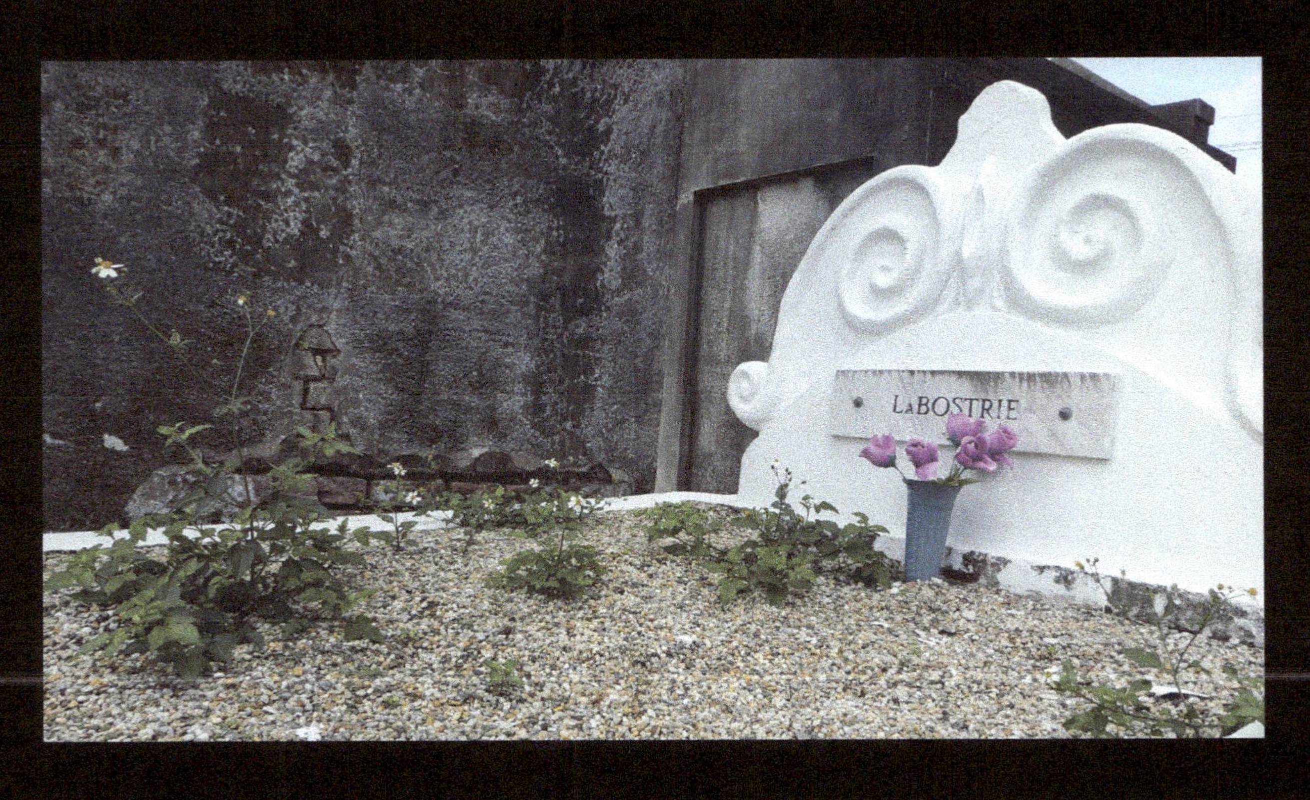

LaBOSTRIE

# OFFERING

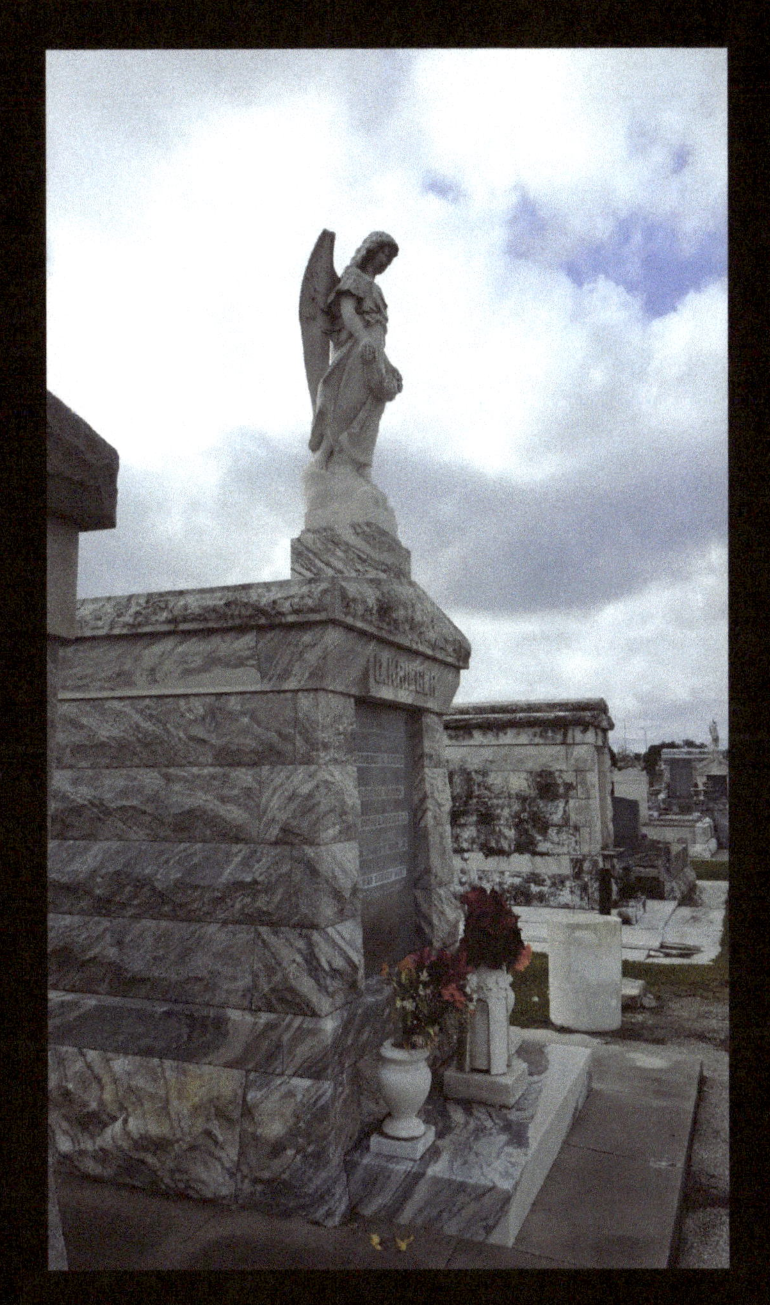

# GREEN AND
# PURPLE FRIENDS

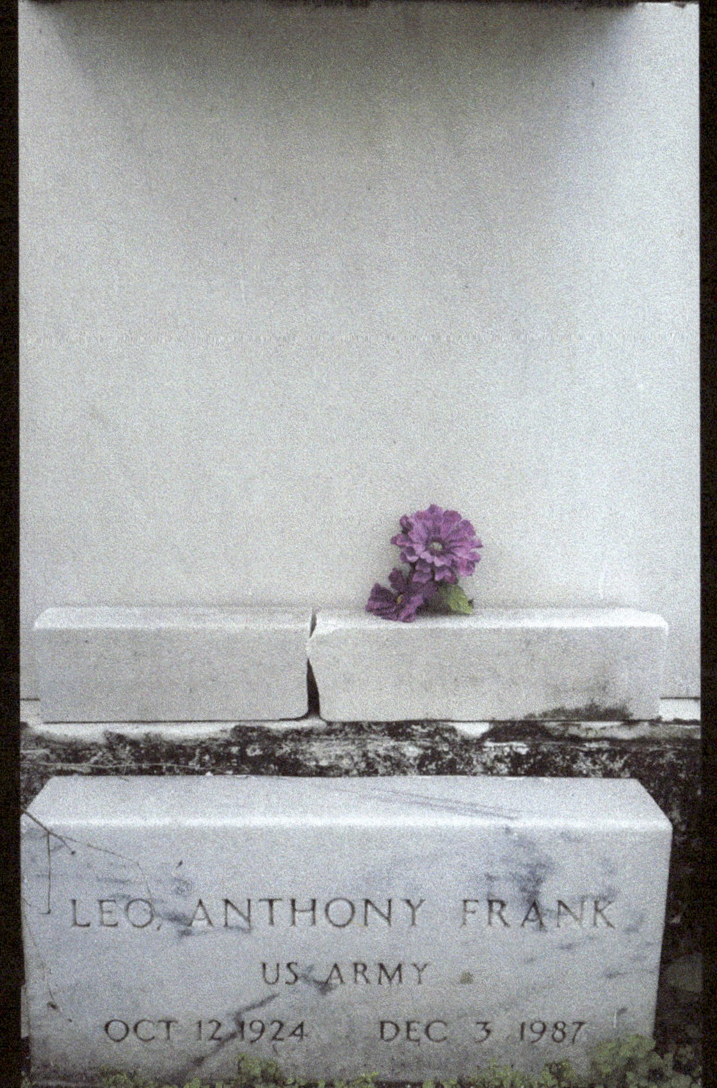

LEO ANTHONY FRANK
US ARMY
OCT 12 1924     DEC 3 1987

# CONDO

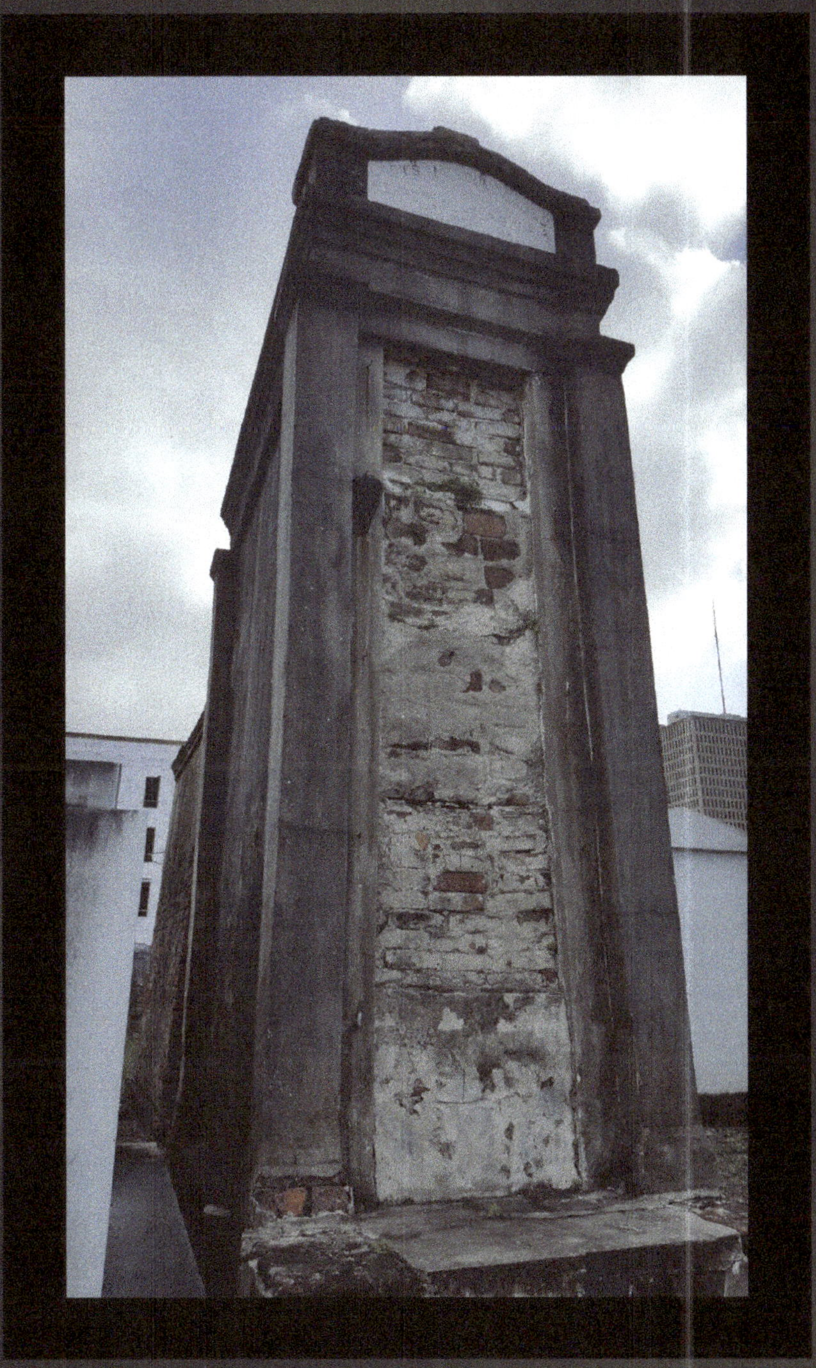

LIFE PERSISTS

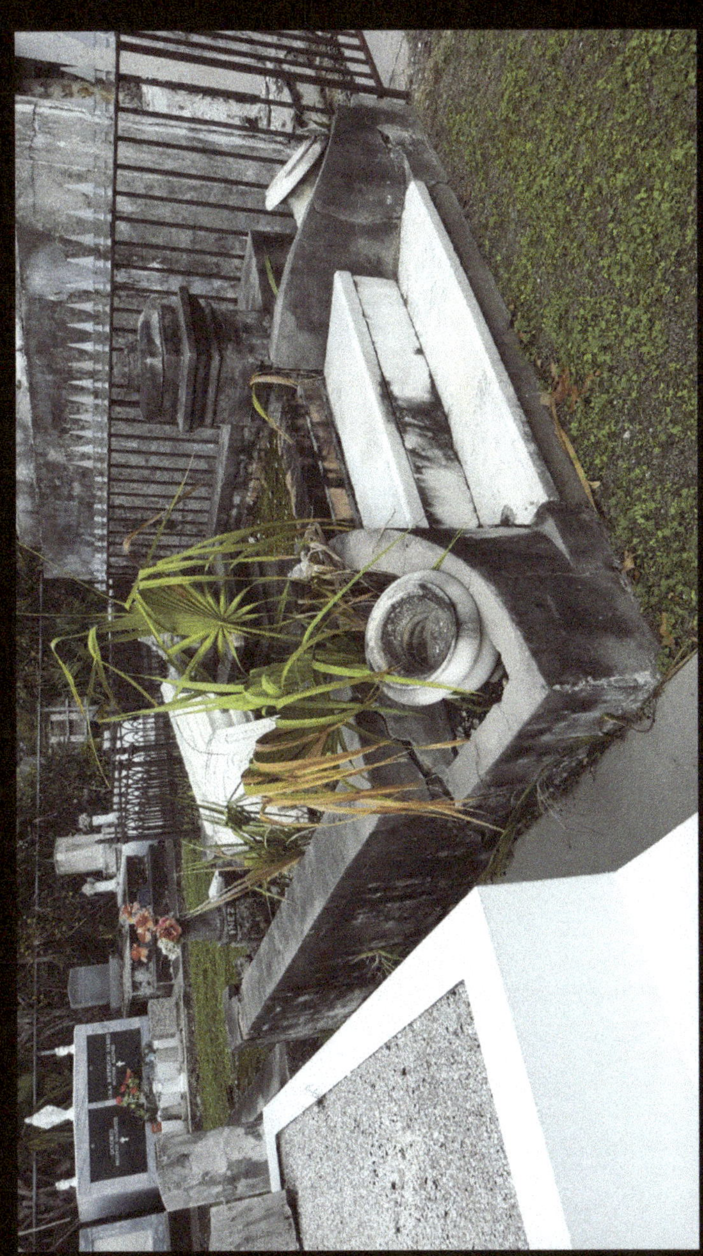

# MERRY BAND OF MISFITS

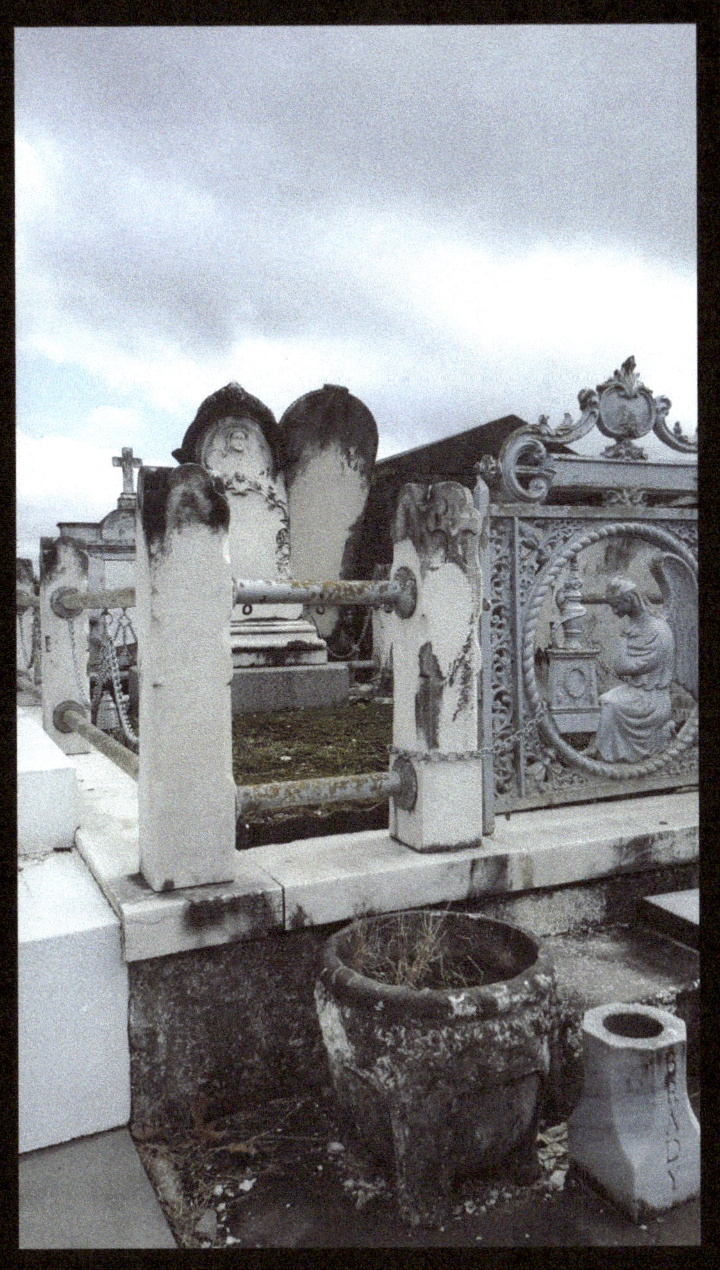

SILVER PALING

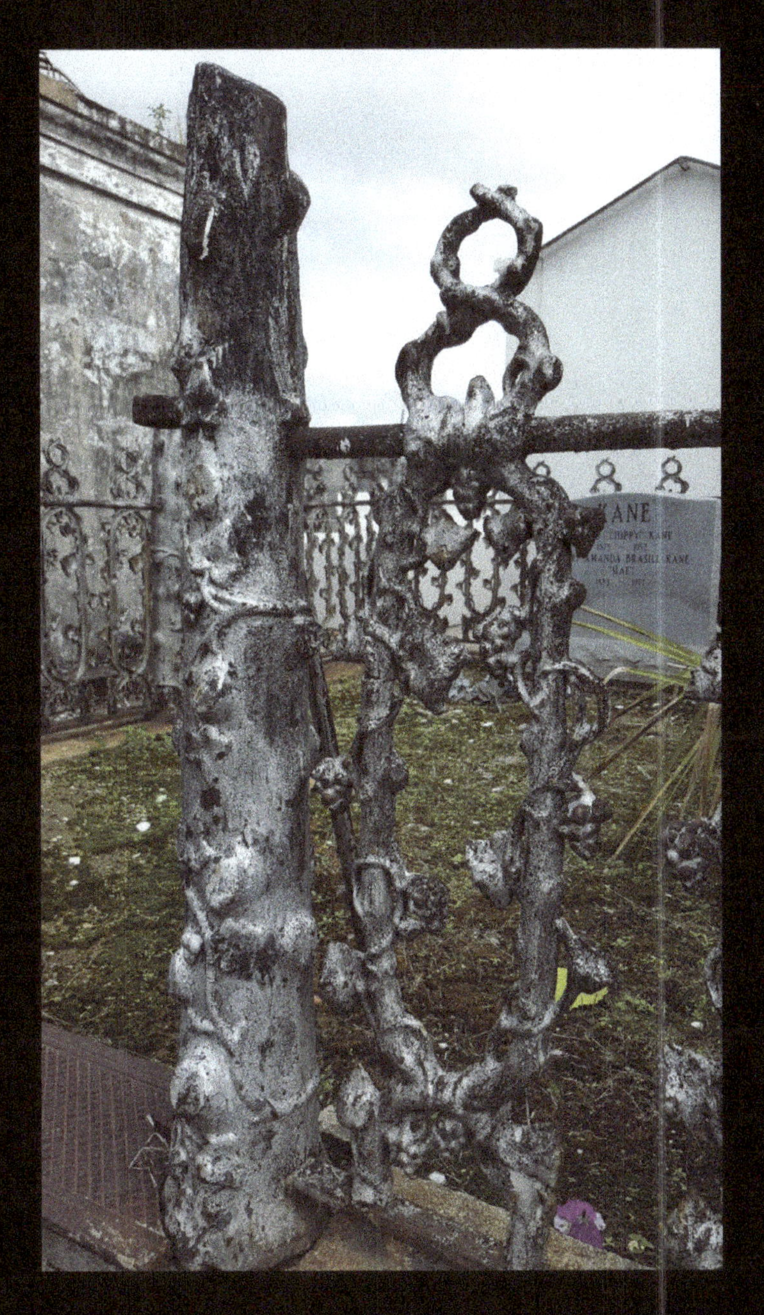

POWER DOWN

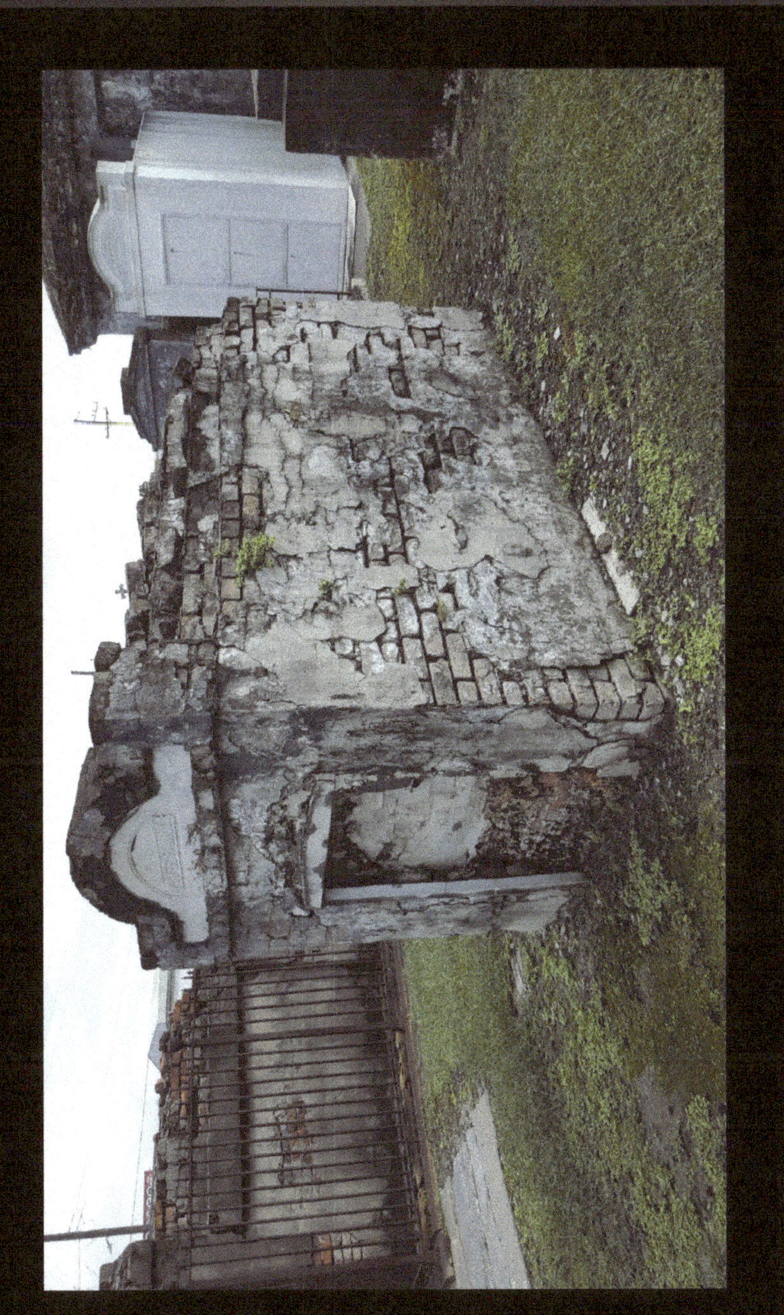

WELCOME

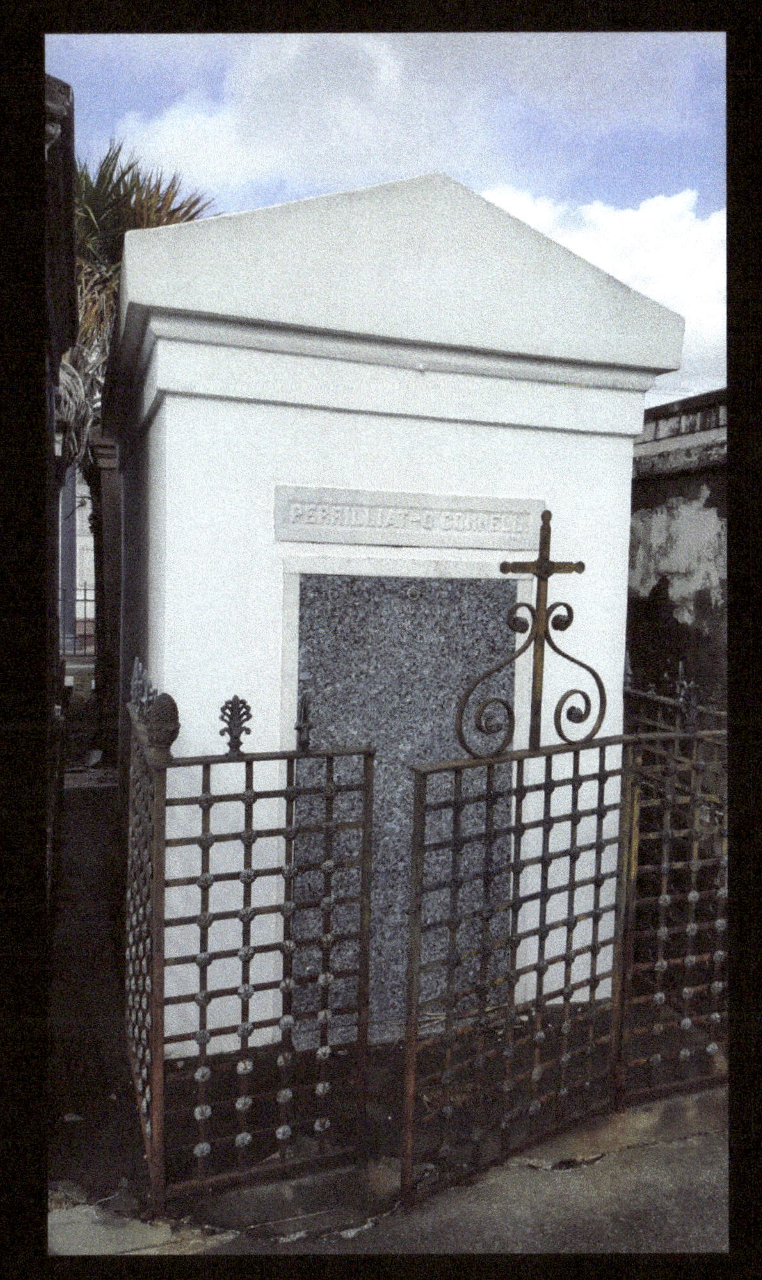

# STOCKADE

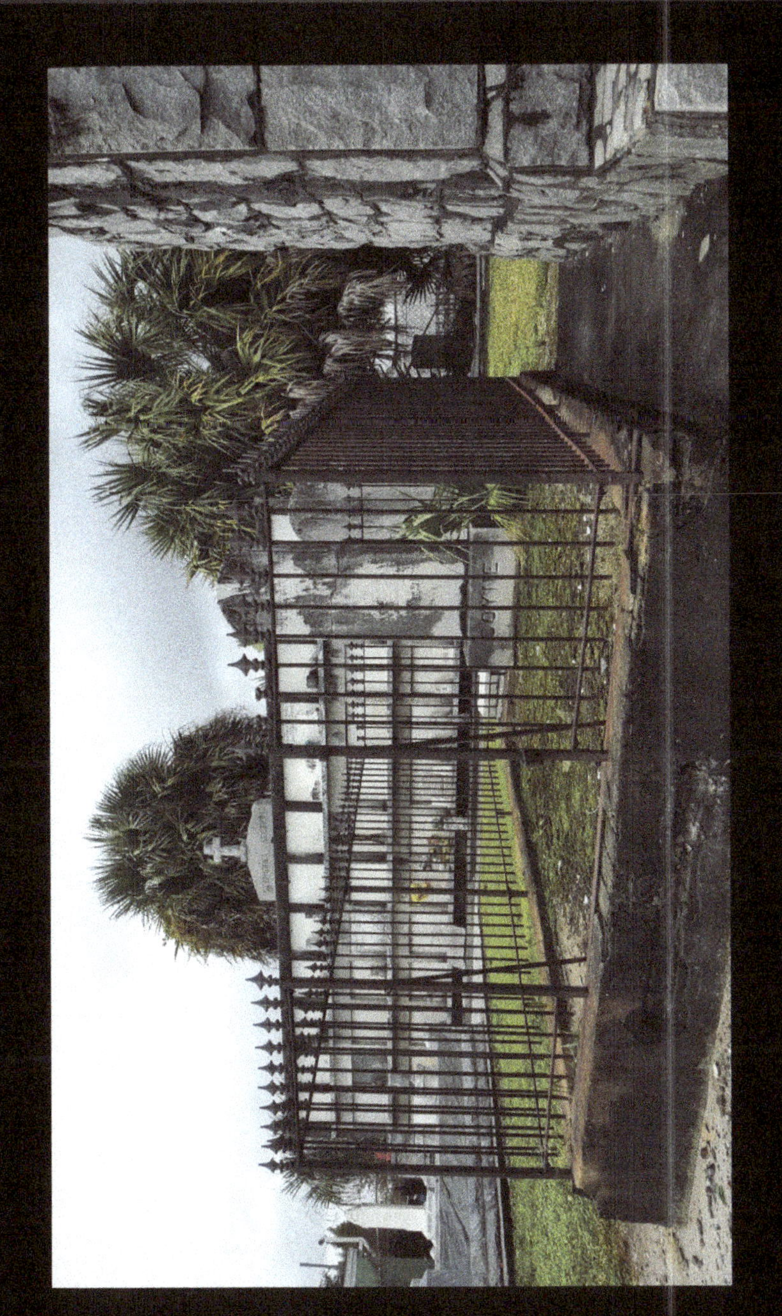

SALOY BIRD

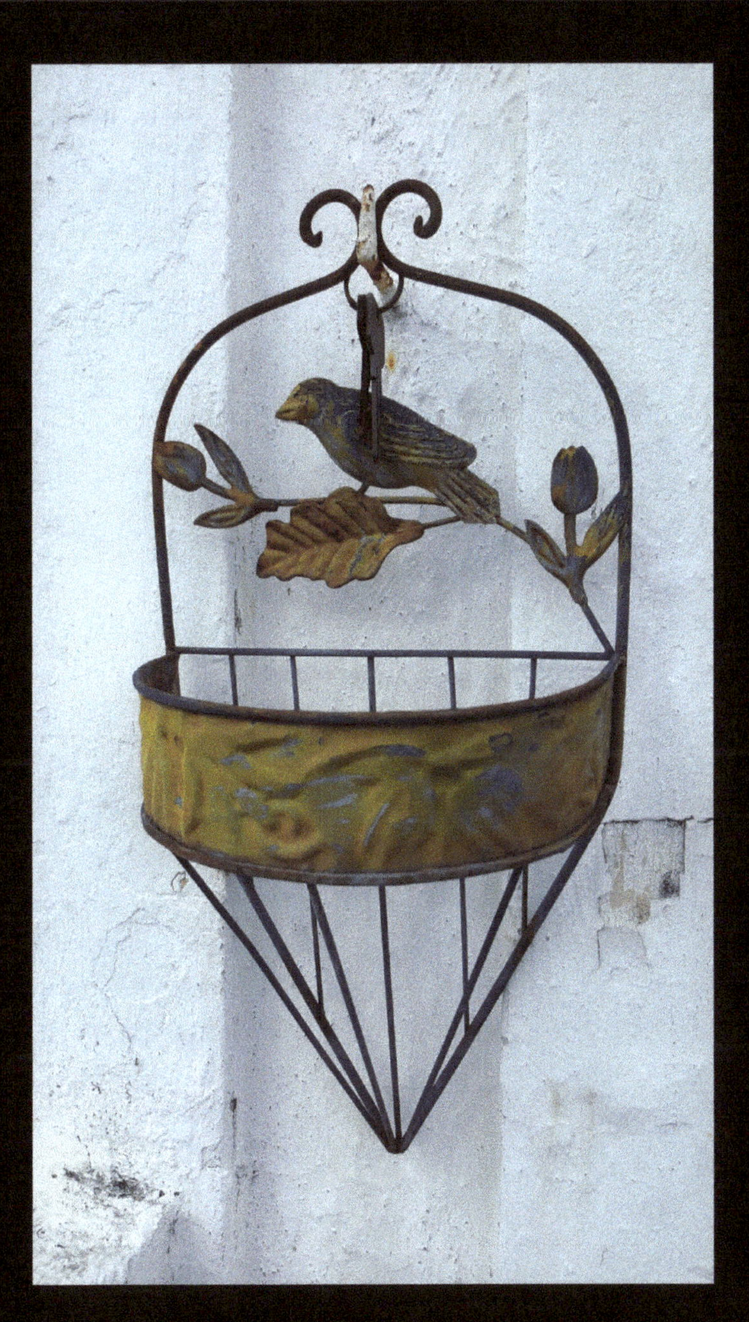

# COBBLESTONE

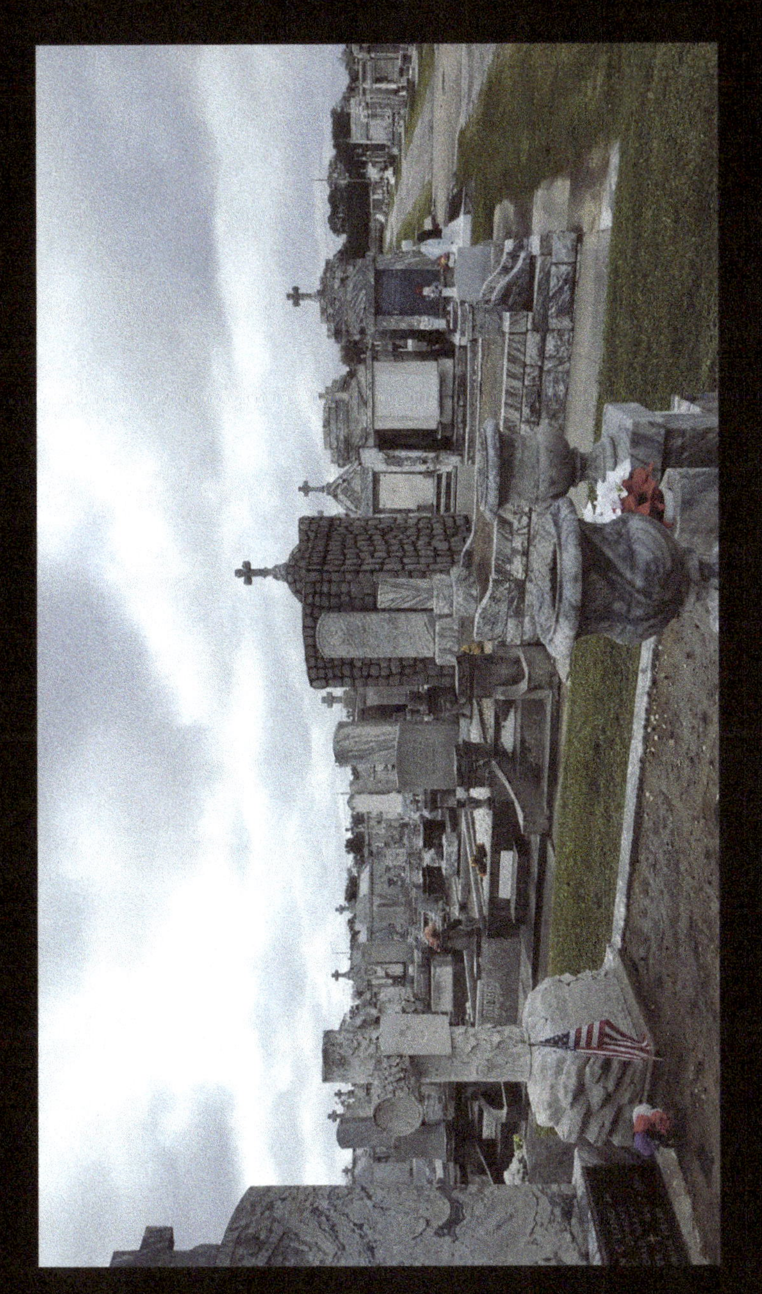

GNOME

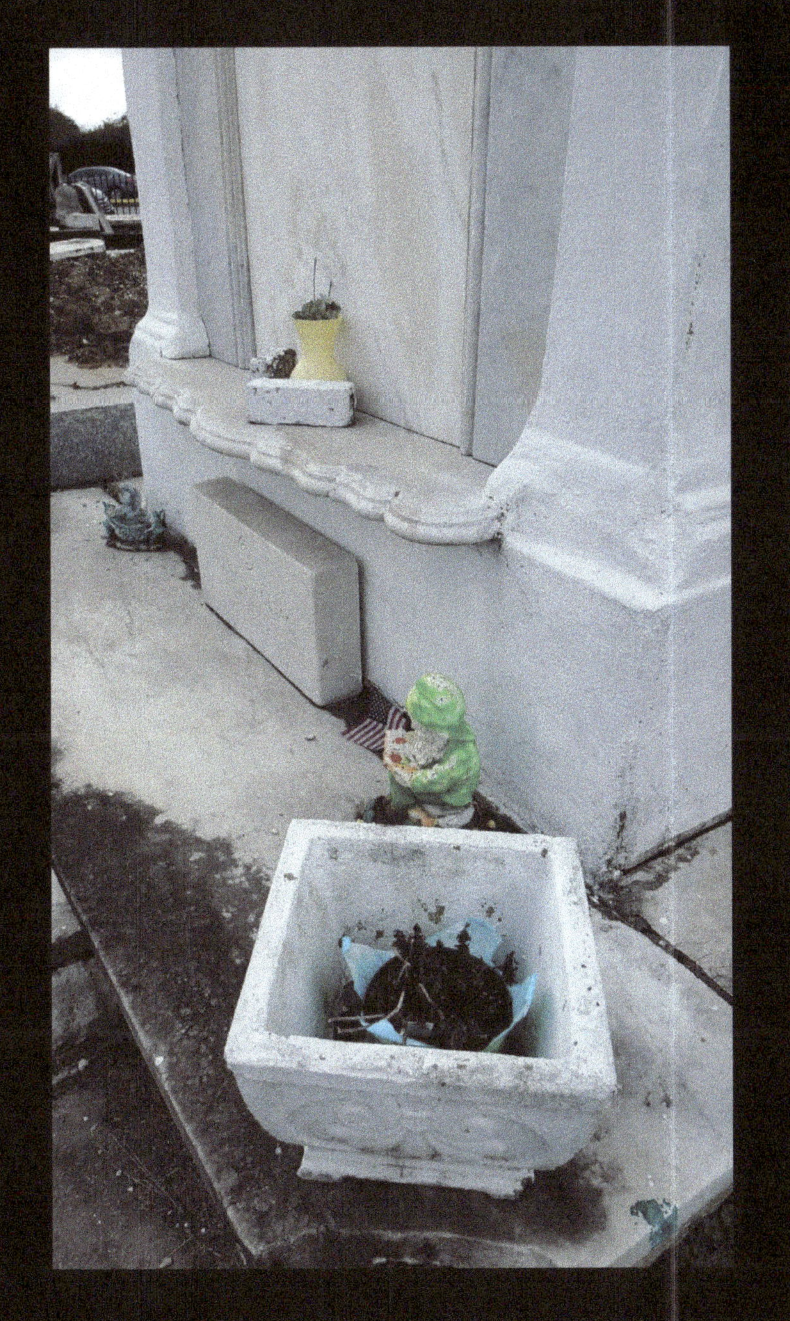

# INTRUSION

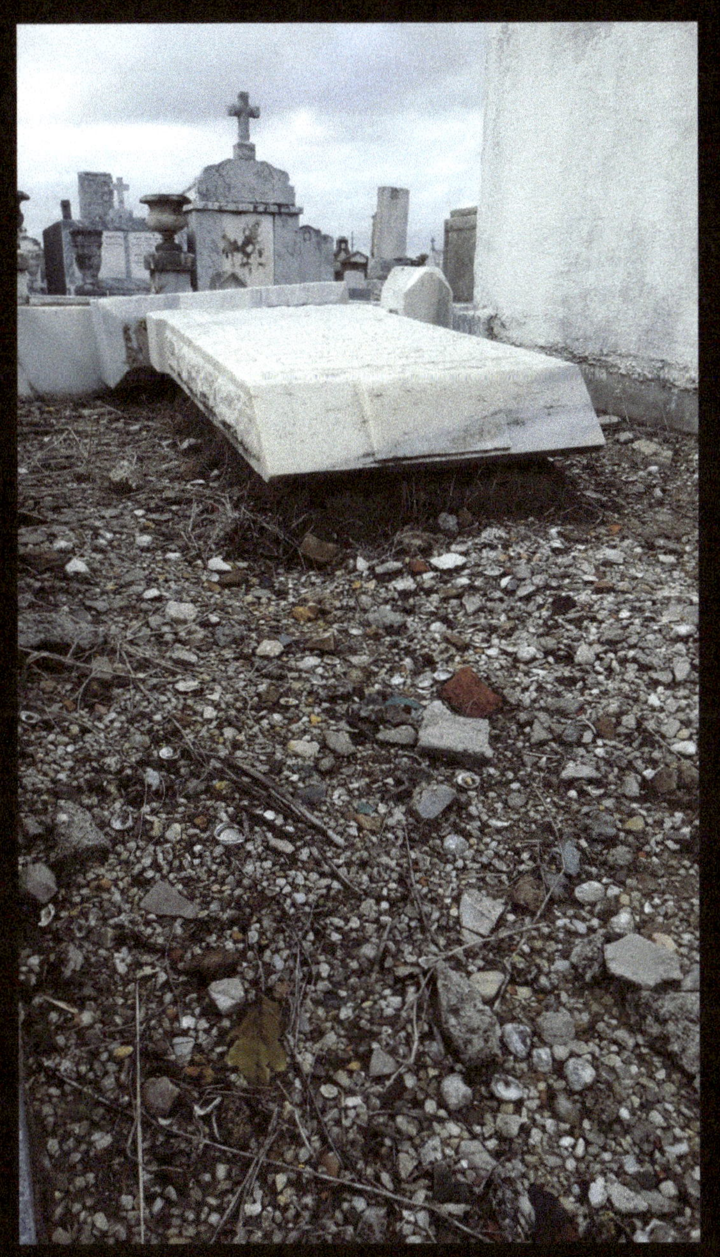

# STEPS OF
# VAN HORSSEN

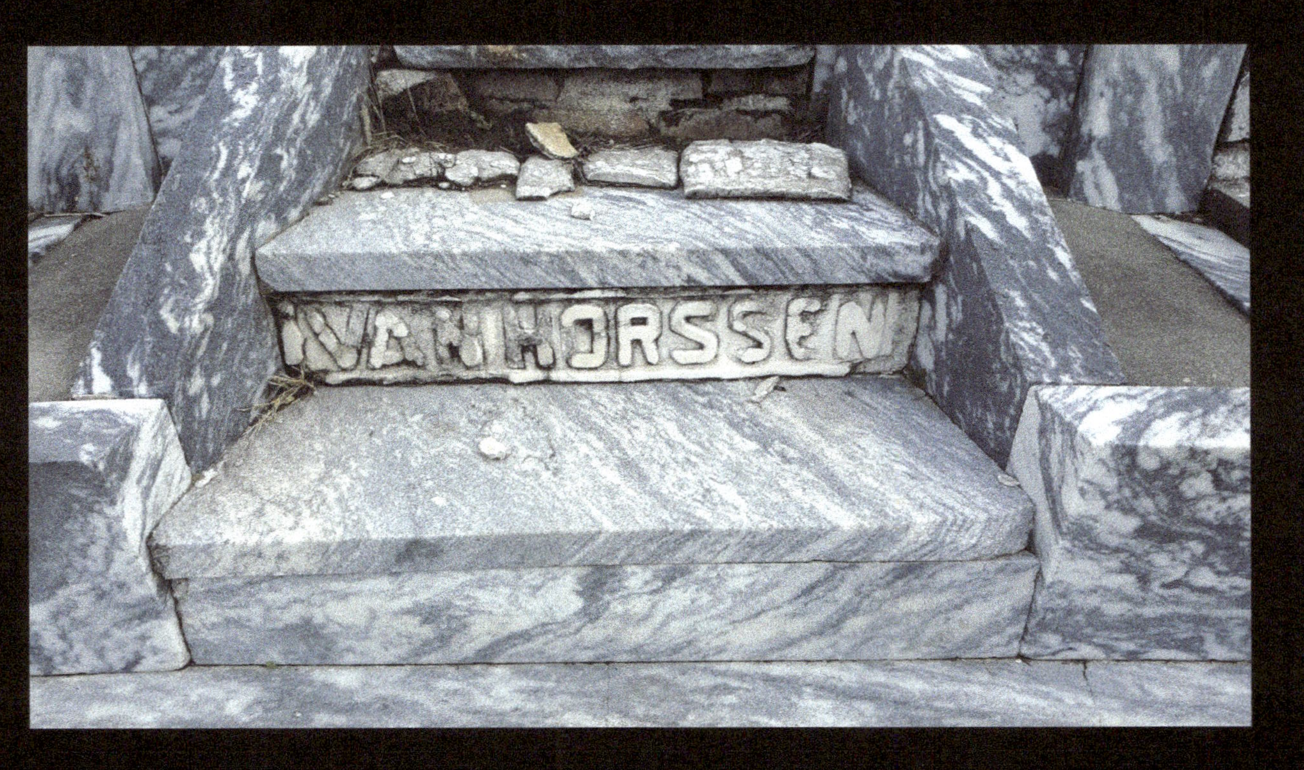
VAN HORSSEN

# FESTOONED

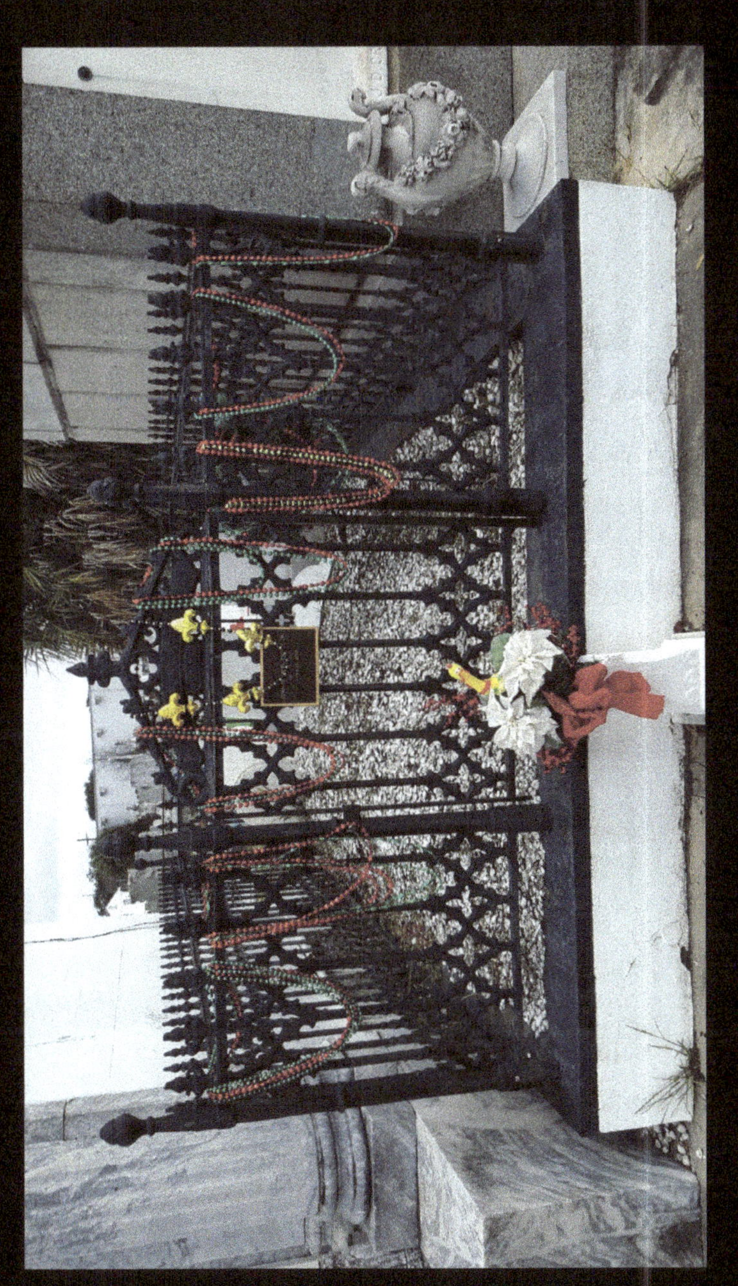

EYES CAST UPWARD

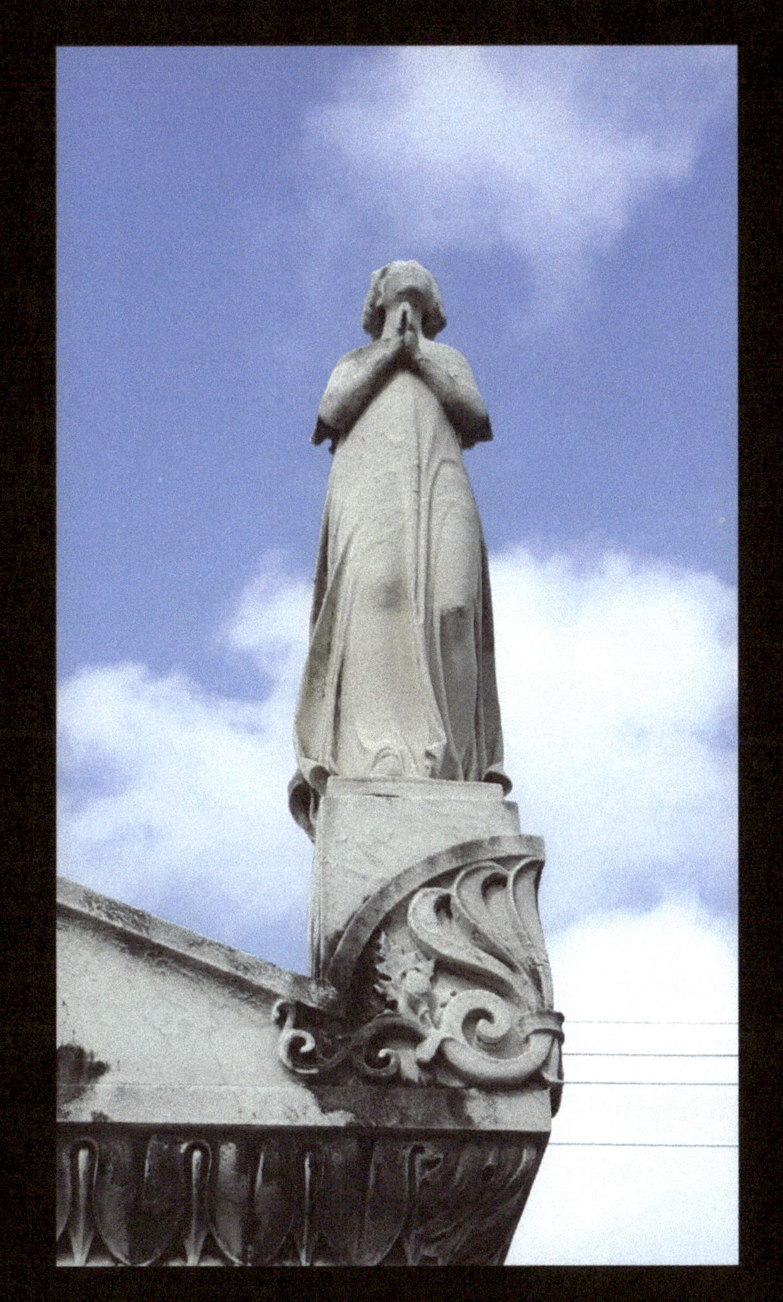

# ALTAR

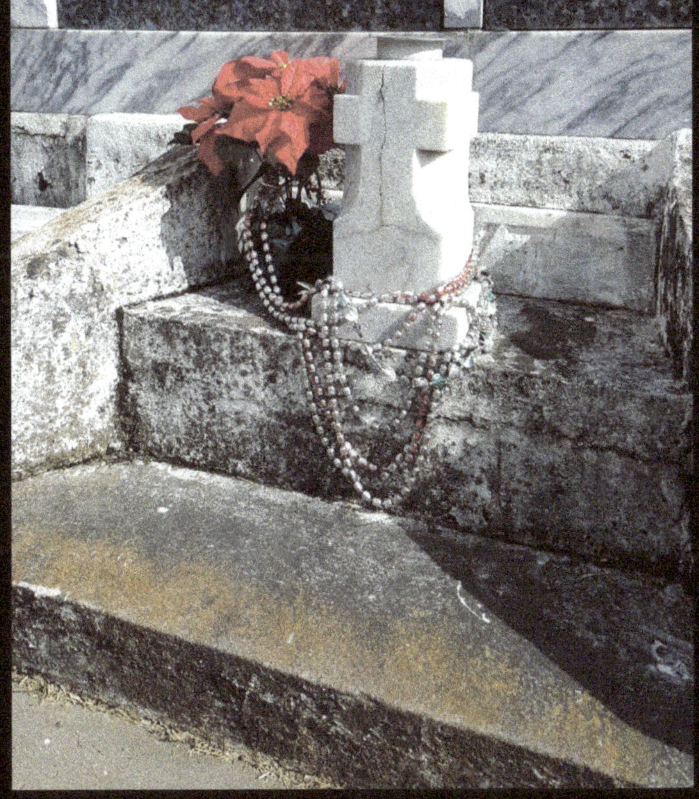

SELMA F. ROBERTS
JOHN W. ROBERTS, SR.
ROBIN M. SHULTZ
ANNIE & ARTHUR ROBERTS
BETTY "D. GROH          1989
ANNIE ROBINA SHULTZ
WILLIAM HARRY GROH
1922                    2009
MAR
NORMA
CATHERIN
CYNTHIA
AUG. 4, 194

# ANGKOR WAT

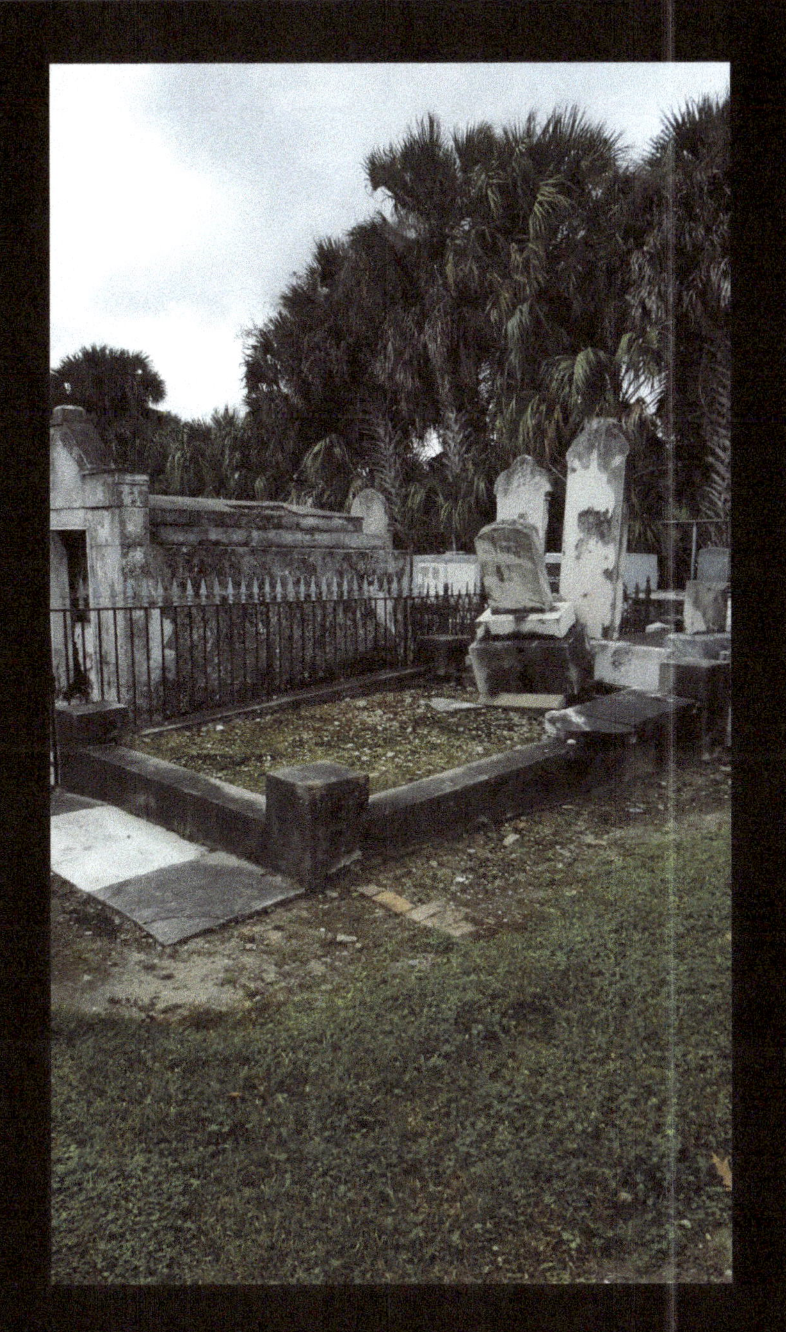

BIBLE HOUSE

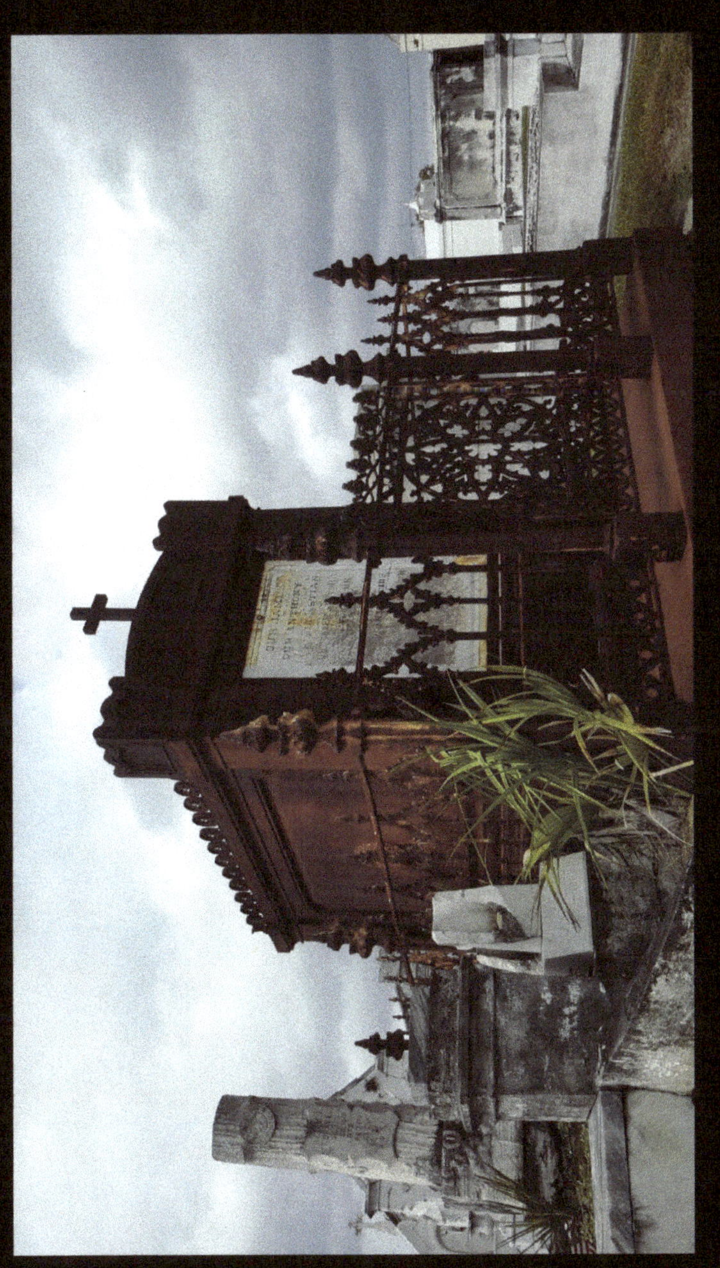

# A HARD RAIN'S
GONNA FALL

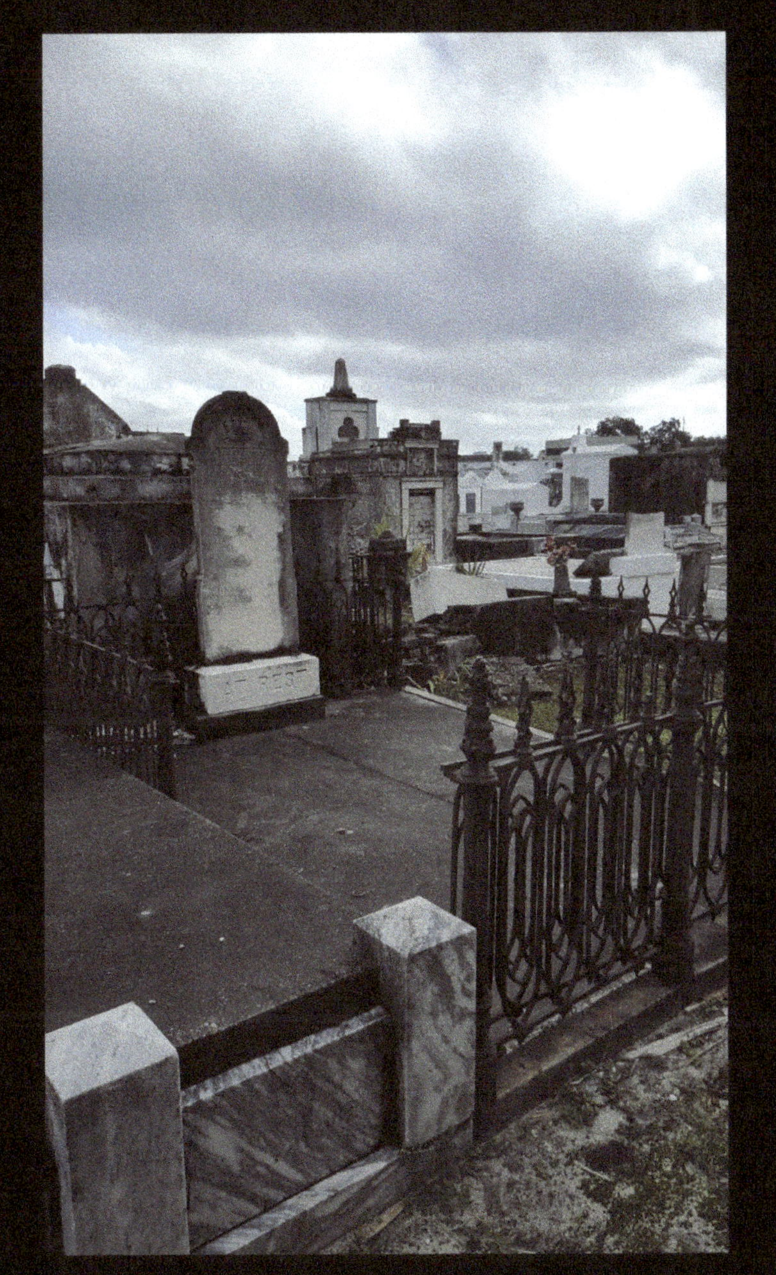

# MONTPLAISIR FAMILY

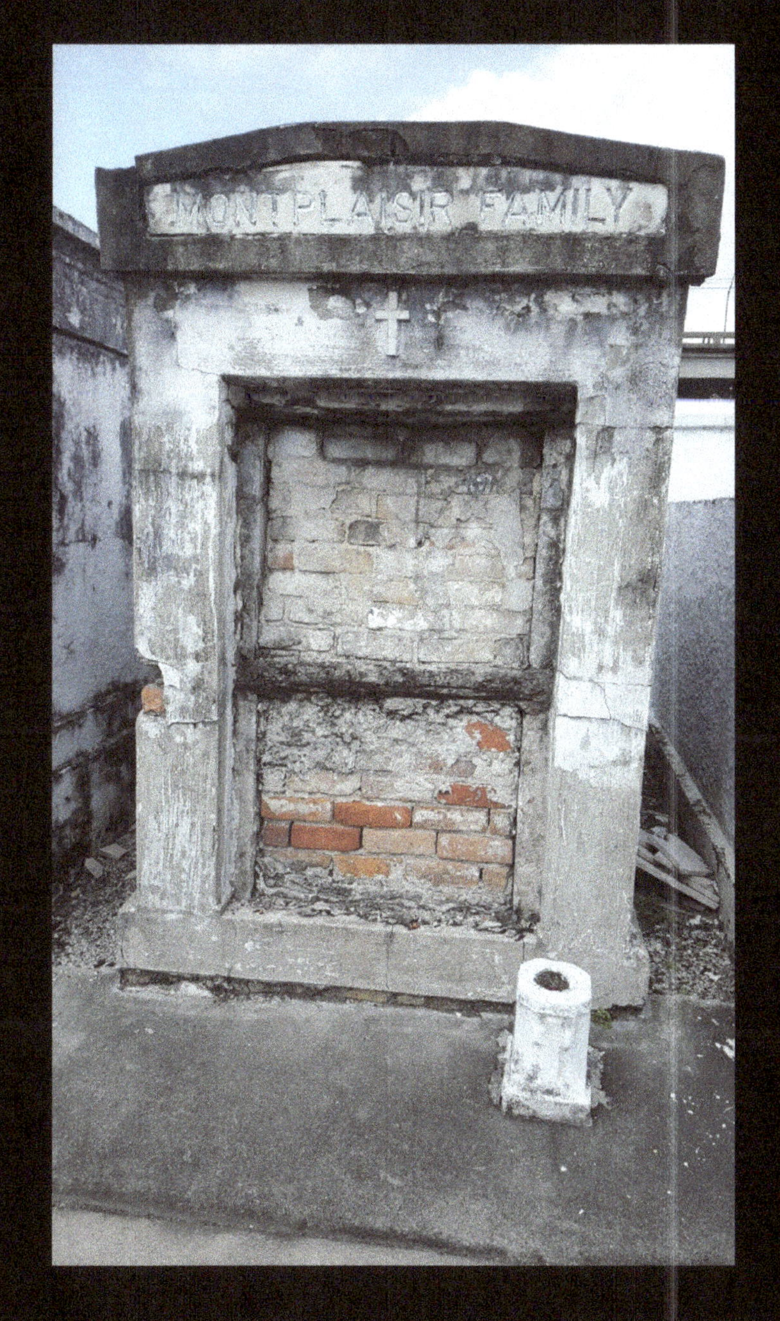
MONTPLAISIR FAMILY

# SALTED BEARDS

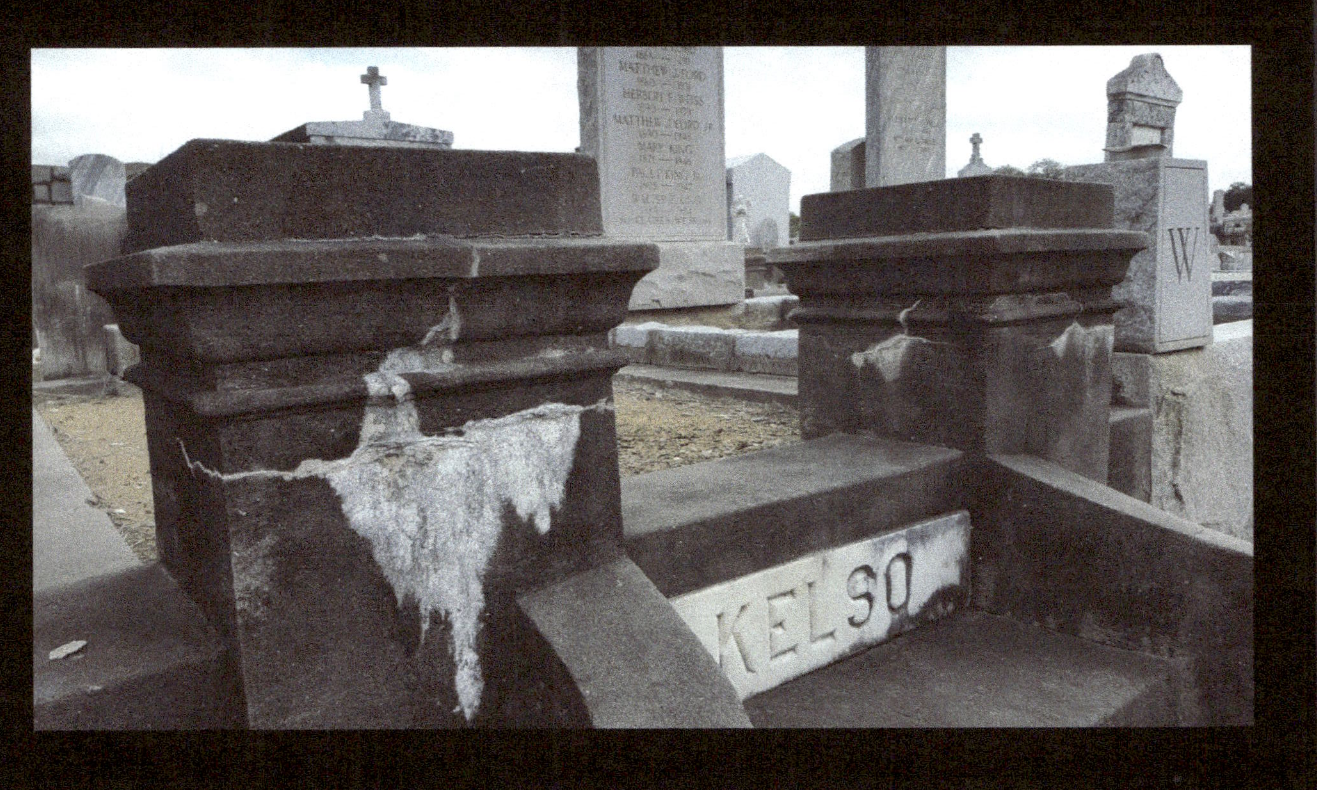
KELSO
W
MATTHEW J FORD
HERBERT F ROSS
MATTHEW J FORD JR
MARY KING
PAUL PRINCE JR

TONGUE

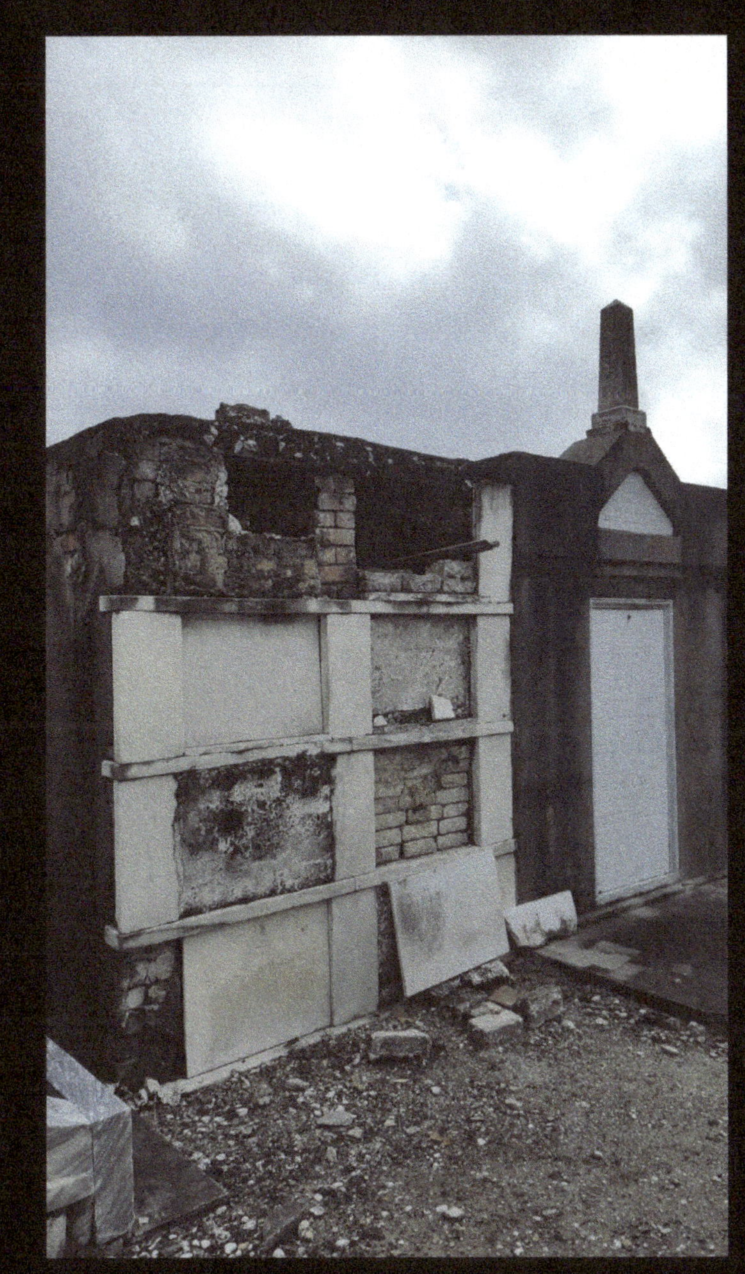

SAMOVAR

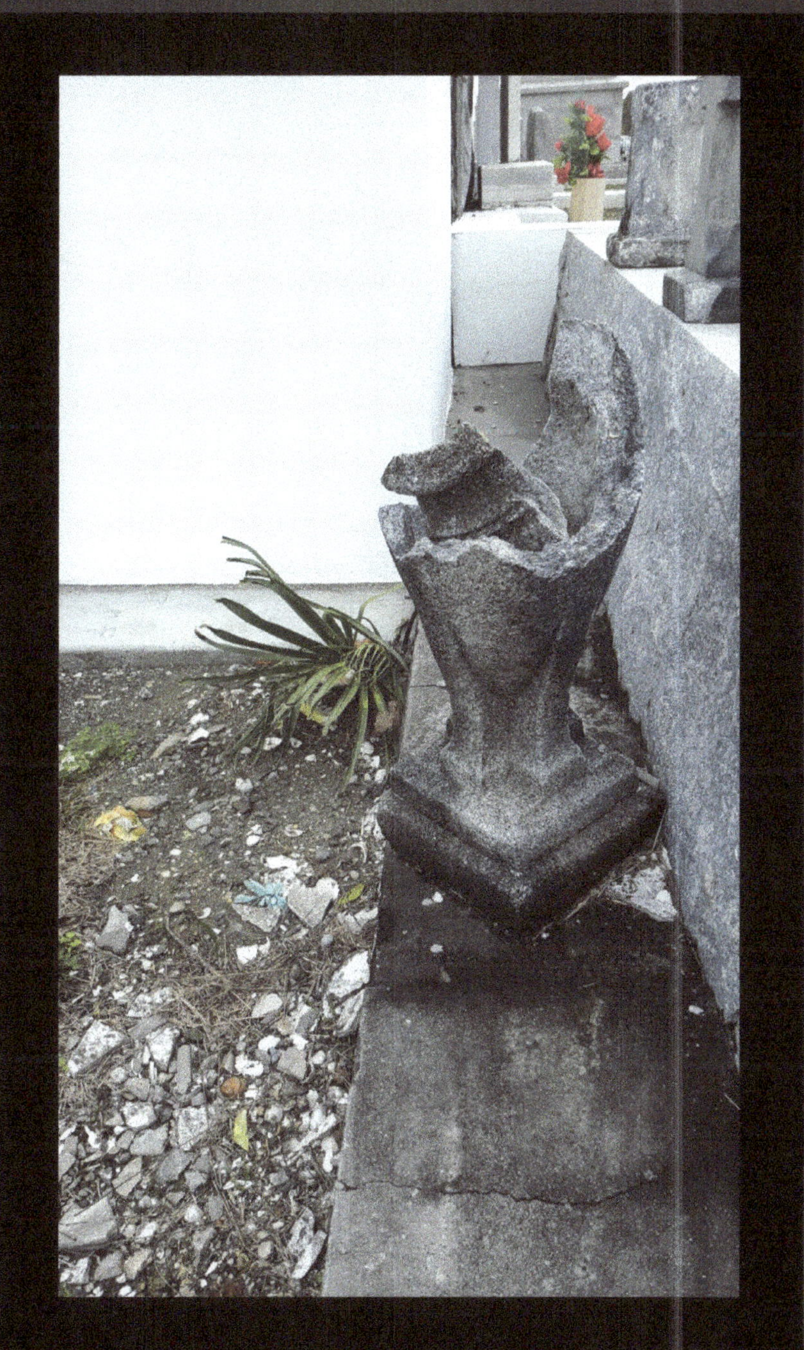

TOWERS

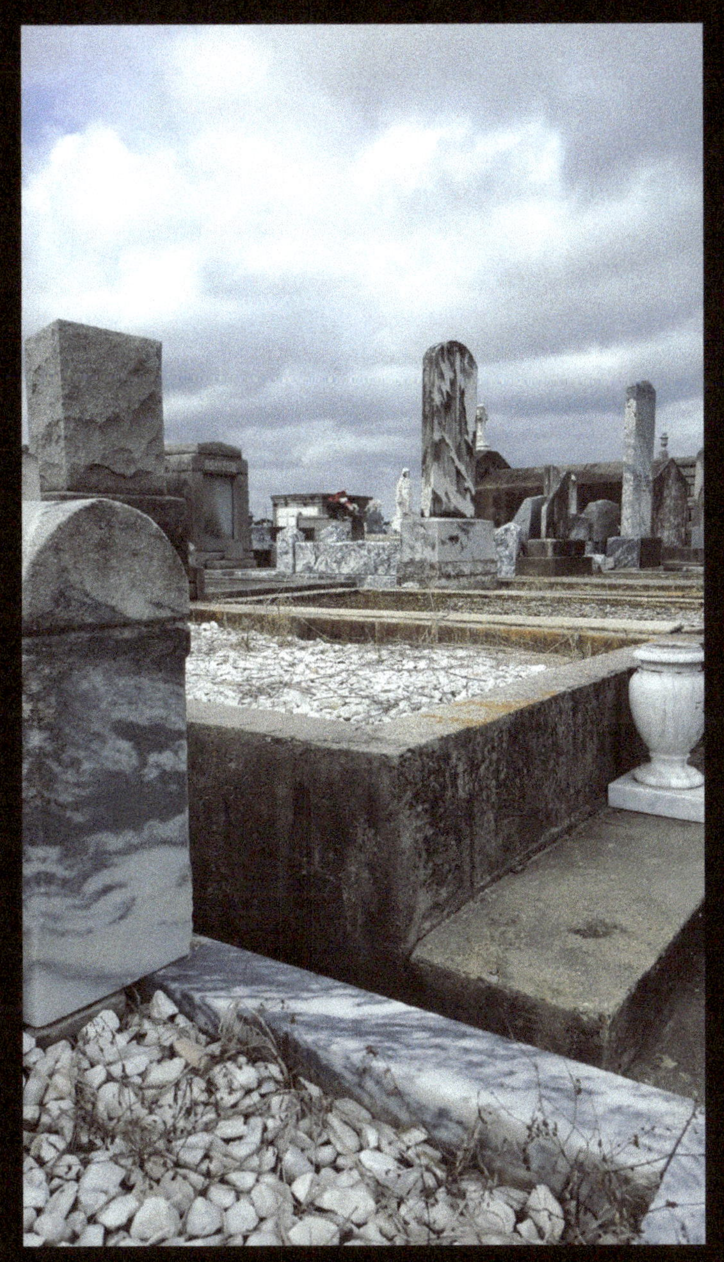

# About the Author

Laine Cunningham is an award-winning novelist whose career takes her around the world for extended stays. She enjoys sharing these special times with readers through the Travel Photo Art series.

**Novels by Laine Cunningham**

*The Family Made of Dust*
*Beloved*
*Reparation*

**Other Books by Laine Cunningham**

*Woman Alone*
*A Six-Month Journey Through the Australian Outback*

The *Woman Alone* Companion Series

*On the Wallaby Track*
*18,000 Miles*
*Fairy Bread and Bush Tucker*
*Amazing Australia*

*Seven Sisters*
*Spiritual Messages from Aboriginal Australia*

*Writing While Female or Black or Gay*
*Diverse Voices in Publishing*

The Zen for Life Series

*The Zen of Travel*
*The Zen of Gardening*
*Zen in the Stable*
*The Zen of Chocolate*
*The Zen of Dogs*

The Wisdom for Life Series

*The Wisdom of Puppies*
*The Wisdom of Babies*
*The Wisdom of Weddings*

The Travel Photo Art Series

*Bikes of Berlin*
*Necropolises of New Orleans I & II*
*Ruins of Rome*
*Ancients of Assisi*
*Panoramas of Portugal*